Forest Walking

Great horned owl, Albro Woods, Rhode Island

Forest Walking

Discovering the Trees
and Woodlands
of North America

Peter Wohlleben
and Jane Billinghurst

GREYSTONE BOOKS
Vancouver/Berkeley/London

Greystone Books Ltd.
greystonebooks.com

Cataloguing data available from Library and Archives Canada
ISBN 978-1-77164-331-3 (pbk.)
ISBN 978-1-77164-332-0 (epub)

Text adapted by Jane Billinghurst
Copyediting by Lynne Melcombe
Proofreading by Stefania Alexandru
Indexing by Stephen Ullstrom
Cover and text design by Jessica Sullivan
Cover and interior photographs by Jane Billinghurst
Map by Emily S. Damstra

Printed and bound in Canada on FSC® certified paper at Friesens. The FSC®
label means that materials used for the product have been responsibly sourced.

Greystone Books gratefully acknowledges the Musqueam, Squamish, and
Tsleil-Waututh peoples on whose land our Vancouver head office is located.

Greystone Books thanks the Canada Council for the Arts,
the British Columbia Arts Council, the Province of British Columbia
through the Book Publishing Tax Credit, and the Government
of Canada for supporting our publishing activities.

Canada

MIX
Paper from
responsible sources
FSC® C016245

BRITISH COLUMBIA

BRITISH COLUMBIA
ARTS COUNCIL
An agency of the Province of British Columbia

Canada Council   Conseil des arts
for the Arts   du Canada

To all who set out to explore a forest,
may you find many wonders and delights

CONTENTS

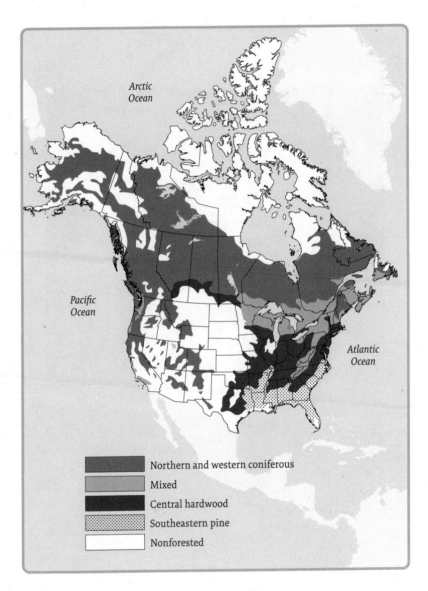

Arctic
Ocean

Pacific
Ocean

Atlantic
Ocean

Northern and western coniferous
Mixed
Central hardwood
Southeastern pine
Nonforested

Main Forest Types in North America

Fallen redwood, Humboldt Redwoods State Park, California

Introduction

WHEN MY PUBLISHER asked me if I wanted to write a book for people to take with them when they went out walking in the forest, I said yes right away. My love for wooded areas has informed most of my choices in life, which is interesting, because I fell into this line of work quite by chance. I originally planned to study biology because, like many high school graduates today, I didn't know how best to channel my love of the natural world. Then my mother came across a small advertisement in the local newspaper from the state forestry commission: they were looking for trainees. I applied, was accepted, and spent the next four years studying the theory and practice of forestry.

As it turned out, the job for which I studied so hard did not come close to fulfilling the dreams I had nurtured for so long. The first problem, which turned out to be the tip of a whole iceberg of problems, was working with heavy machinery, which destroys the forest floor. This was followed by using insecticides that kill on contact, clearcutting, and cutting down the oldest trees (the ancient beeches I love so much). I found these tasks increasingly worrisome. Over the course of my studies, I had been taught that these practices were necessary to ensure the health of the forest. It might amaze you to learn that there are still thousands of students who believe their professors when they pass down these same lessons. My discomfort soon turned to horror, and I didn't know how I was going to survive a career in forestry.

In 1991, I was lucky enough to find a community that shared my values. Located in the Eifel mountains in Germany, the community of Hümmel owned forestlands and wanted to manage them sustainably. Together we created a plan that included a mix of uses, including parcels to be left untouched and parcels where resources would be extracted carefully to minimize impacts. The guiding principle behind our plan was to involve the community in the decision-making process. I designed several activities to help us achieve our goals. Survival-training weekends and building log cabins were the most adventurous. Mostly, I led guided tours through the wonderful world of trees.

After the tours, people often asked me where they could read up on what they had just learned. I could only shrug, as I did not know of any books on the subject. My wife kept pressuring me to put something in writing for visitors to take home with them. And so, while on vacation in Lapland, I committed to paper what I would talk about on a typical guided tour. I sent the text off to several publishers and told my wife: "If no one agrees to publish my book by the end of the year, writing is clearly not for me."

As you can tell from the book you now hold, that is not what happened. Since the publication of my first book, *The Hidden Life of Trees*, I have found great joy in expanding what I do. Now I can get many more people excited about forests because, in my opinion, forests are not being used nearly as much as they should be. I'm not talking about the depredations of the timber industry, which does altogether too much in too many places. I'm talking about the adventures, great and small, waiting to be discovered amongst the trees. And to find them, there's just one thing you need to do: take a walk in a forest. I am so happy that Jane Billinghurst, my longtime English translator, has come along on this journey to help point out the amazing variety of adventures to be found in forests in North America.

BEFORE WE SET OUT, it might be helpful for you to know what I mean by the word "forest." The trees most of us know best are lined up in rows along city streets, set out in tasteful arrangements in urban parks, or displayed as exotic specimens in arboretums.

I'm sure you've all seen sidewalks buckling as tree roots push up from underground. Or noticed the cages around trunks to protect them from passersby. Or heard about trees whose roots have penetrated water pipes, leading to the miscreants' swift removal. Trees in urban areas that are not removed for bad behavior are usually cut back to keep them neat, tidy, and safe for pedestrians walking beneath them.

Life for trees in parks and in arboretums is a little better, but not much. There are often just one or two of the same species and they may well be growing far from home, struggling in conditions that are new to them. They do not have an extended family to support them, and they grow old without ever having the opportunity to watch a new generation grow up around them.

When I talk about a forest, I'm not talking about rows of trees in urban settings or individuals in parks. I'm talking about a large group of trees growing together. But are all large stands of trees away from cities necessarily forests? I trained as a forester. My job was to go out into what I thought of as a forest to look at individual trees and evaluate them for their economic potential. What was important was how straight they grew and how free they were from pests and diseases.

I now understand that the places where I worked were not forests, but tree plantations, where trees of mostly the same age and species are planted in rows so they are easy to maintain and harvest. These trees are often planted in places where they would not naturally grow. If one of them falls or dies, it is removed. Harvest is timed to maximize profits, and the trees are cut down before they have a chance to grow old.

When I talk of the forest, I'm talking about a community. In a forest left to its own devices, trees of different ages and different species grow in the places they choose and that suit them best. Huge mother trees provide their children with the conditions they need to grow up slowly, which leads to strong, healthy individuals. Trees may live for hundreds (even thousands) of years before they finally die and fall to the forest floor.

Dead trees are as important to the forest as living trees. Indeed, they are even more important. Standing dead trees provide homes for woodpeckers first, and then the owls and other birds and animals that move in after the woodpeckers move out. Soil exposed when a great tree tips over provides an open space for seeds to land and start to grow, and the massive root structure offers hiding places for small mammals. Finally, an army of decomposers breaks the wood of the fallen tree down into nutrients for the next generation.

The clean-up crew's task is not complete until the last remnants of wood have rotted away. Then, the remains of the trees and the creatures that processed them slip deep into the earth, taking their stores of carbon with them and locking them safely away.

The forest is so closely linked to place that the trees themselves begin to shape the soil, the climate, the frequency of fire, and the path taken by water in the surrounding landscape.

~ 1 ~

Total
Immersion

AS SOON AS YOU step into a forest, you step into a different space. Depending on the type of forest, the trees may be growing together so closely that their tops almost touch. Outside, the sun may be shining brightly, but here, you are in the shade. The leaves are busily absorbing sunlight to make food. What little light makes it through the canopy is mostly green, so it feels as though you are slipping into an underwater world.

The forest is refreshingly cool. Years of discarded leaves and needles have turned the ground into a huge sponge that absorbs rainwater as it drips through the leaves and then slowly releases it into the forest floor. Above ground, you breathe in damp air, while below ground, the trees tap into the pockets of moisture captured by their maze of roots after the last rains fell. Fallen branches and trunks lie strewn on the forest floor. Rain-saturated rotting wood and downed logs steam as the sun hits them. The trees, both living and dead, are actively creating the cool, shady, moist conditions they most enjoy.

Let your eyes adjust to the quality of light around you and listen as the breeze brushes through the branches. It sounds like traffic on a distant highway, water cascading over rocks, or waves breaking on the shore. Individual trees creak and groan as they rub against one another, each producing a slightly different sound depending on how slowly or quickly, how densely or airily their wood has grown. You might even hear a hollow tree humming as though it's experimenting with the beginnings of a tune.

Leaves and needles whisper and sing. Dry leaves hanging on young beeches chatter in the brisk spring air while they wait for the larger trees in the forest to leaf out. Unfolded aspen leaves produce a muffled muttering as the breeze turns them one way and then the other. The stems of most leaves are round to keep the tops of the leaves oriented to the sun, but the stems of aspen leaves are flat, allowing the leaves to twist in the wind so both sides can bathe in the light. Vortices of air form around and detach from the tips of conifer needles, producing a melodic chorus—known in Japanese as *matsukase* or the "song of the pines"—that varies in pitch as the breeze builds and dies. Small branches buffeted against one another twang like wire strung taut between fence posts. On a hot day, the popping of pinecones opening and ejecting their seeds punctuates this symphony of sound.

If you are one of those people who has trouble slowing down to listen, you might pick up on the soundtrack of the forest when something quite different draws your attention. As Jane took photographs of a particularly pleasing pattern of lichens on bark in Big Thicket National Preserve in Texas, she heard a rustling. Quite a loud rustling, it seemed to her, but when she investigated, she discovered it came from a small brown grasshopper perfectly blended into the leaf litter below. If she had not been stopped and silent at that moment, she would never have noticed it, even though it was right at her feet. It froze as she bent down to inspect it.

Jane is no entomologist, so she had no idea what kind of grasshopper it was, but a search back home revealed it to be the delightfully named "mischievous bird grasshopper"— also known, somewhat less delightfully, as the Carolina locust.

As humans, we rely heavily on visual images and are not particularly skilled at interpreting sounds, especially in unfamiliar territory. In forests where bears are about, birds scratching in leaf litter can sound especially large and menacing. Later in her trip, Jane, who lives in the Pacific Northwest, heard a quiet mewing sound in Highlands Hammock State Park near Sebring, Florida, and became convinced it must be a panther kitten calling for its mother. It turned out to be a gray squirrel hiding behind a branch. A mysterious nocturnal scuffling around her campsite in Paynes Prairie Preserve State Park just south of Gainesville revealed itself in the comforting light of morning to have been an armadillo snuffling for insects in the thick layer of leaves under the live oaks.

Because we rely so heavily on sight, the merest flicker of movement quickly commands our attention even if an animal is being as quiet as it can be. In the beech-magnolia forests of southern Texas and the baldcypress swamps of northern Florida, these movements often come from green anoles scattering at the sound of your approach. Jane watched one skittering across a boardwalk in the Okefenokee Swamp Park in Georgia. On the boardwalk it was a dull brown, but as soon as it reached the grassy vegetation on the other side, it turned a bright, almost luminous, green. She had witnessed the so-called American chameleon in action.

Stopping to listen hones your senses until even stationary patterns register: a black-and-yellow salamander by the side of the trail, an orb-weaver spider suspended between branches (careful you don't walk into its web), a striped chipmunk standing on guard next to a small crevice at the base of a tree. As you walk through the forest, many eyes will be watching you. If you take the time to stop and listen, every once in a while, you might discover some of the creatures that have you in their sights.

While you're standing there, taking in the forest, close your eyes. Smell is not exactly our strongest sense, but we become more aware of smells when we are not distracted by what we can see. Some of the aromas you are detecting are being produced by trees as they pass chemical messages amongst themselves. What kind of messages might these be?

Trees, as you have probably noticed, cannot run from danger, so they have other ways of defending themselves. You might get a whiff of a cyanide compound in black cherry bark that smells like bitter almonds. This warning scent lets browsers know not to mess with this tree.

Oaks go even further, using airborne messages to summon reinforcements that help them combat pests. When caterpillars start munching on them, the trees pump bitter tannins into their leaves. They also send chemical messages over the air waves. Parasitic wasps fly in when they receive the oaks' airborne invitations and lay their eggs in the caterpillars. When the eggs hatch, the wasp larvae eat their way out of their hosts, putting an end to the caterpillar buffet.

In a coniferous forest, you will pick up on that piney scent so popular with companies that make room and car deodorizers. It smells like a mixture of sap, candied orange peel, and sugar. It reminds me of summer holidays spent on the coast of the Mediterranean where the pines smell just the same. Many conifers native to northern climes suffer when they are planted in lower latitudes where the weather is too hot and dry for them. When conifers don't have enough to drink, they become stressed because lack of moisture weakens their defenses against bark beetles. They release olfactory alarm signals to warn their companions, and these are the tangy scents that smell so strongly of beach vacations (to me, anyway).

These piney scents come from bitter-tasting essential oils called "terpenes." In spring, pines pump more terpenes into the tender new growth deer prefer to eat and less to old growth that deer tend to avoid. In addition to acting as a deer deterrent because they taste bad, terpenes have antimicrobial and antibacterial qualities that clean the air in the forest, making it pleasant for us to breathe when we decide to indulge in a bit of forest bathing, which is basically like taking a refreshing shower in forest air.

Terpenes are also an essential component of conifer resin. When you see drops of resin oozing down a tree, you know the spruce, fir, or pine is actively defending itself, flushing out intruders such as bark beetles and filling the holes they bore with sticky sap so the beetles cannot crawl inside. I can tell you from experience that if you want to take the weight off your feet or get extra support when crossing a rocky patch in the trail, it's not a good idea to lean on a sticky conifer as it's almost impossible to get the resin off your skin and clothes. Out on the trail, you can try rubbing sticky skin on tree bark to remove as much sap as you can. You'll find some of the dust on the bark sticks to the sap. Now your skin will be dirty, but at least it won't be sticky any longer. Your clothes, alas, will need to wait for more intense treatment when you get home.

Conifers use terpenes in other ways. On hot days, the trees increase their production of terpenes until they rise in the heat to float above the forest, where they attract water molecules. The gathering water molecules form clouds that shade the forest like an enormous sun umbrella. If there is enough moisture around, the trees might even summon up a raincloud or two. It is terpenes that put the "smoky" in Tennessee's Great Smoky Mountains as clouds collect over the forested hillsides.

Not all the scents floating around you are defensive. Some are associated with reproduction. Many forest trees are wind pollinated. Alders hang their catkins in the breeze and pines release puffs of pollen from the pinkish-red pollen cones growing at the tips of their branches. The wind provides an efficient distribution service, dusting neighboring trees with male pollen that fertilizes female reproductive organs to start the next generation. You will get dusted, too. If you suffer from allergies, what is a cause for celebration for the pines and Douglas firs will make you reach for a paper tissue or an antihistamine.

Some forest trees, however, need to attract the attention of insects to make reproduction happen. Insects get a light coating of pollen as they crawl into the trees' flowers in search of pollen and the co-opted carriers then drop off some of the dusty grains at their next floral stop. In forests in the American South, black tupelo trees, magnolias, and black cherries all vie for the pollinators' attention. In the swamp forests of Georgia and central Florida, bees produce highly prized tupelo honey after visiting the flowers of white tupelo trees.

Flowers are eye-catching, but to get ahead of the game, these trees also make their blooms fragrant to let pollinators know energy-rich food is on offer. Scientists at the University of Tel Aviv have discovered that at least one plant, the evening primrose, increases the concentration of sugar in its nectar when bees buzz by. Perhaps some of the sweet forest aromas you smell are coming from trees keeping an ear open for passing pollinators and stepping up sugar production to lure in customers.

If you are out on a mild, damp fall day, you might become aware of an earthy smell that comes not from the trees but the forest floor. This smell is released as springtails and millipedes, bacteria and fungi break down rotten wood and discarded leaves and process the nutrients they contain, making them available to the next generation of forest dwellers. The earthy aroma intensifies after a rain when the force of raindrops hitting the ground splashes bacterial spores up into the air. The smell is most intense after a dry period when spores have been collecting in the soil. We, as humans, are exquisitely attuned to it. We even have a special name for it: petrichor. Perhaps we find it so attractive because it smells like plenty, the promise of new life about to begin.

When you first stepped into the forest, you might have thought you were the most active organism around, but as you can see, the forest itself constantly reacts to and shapes its environment, from the air above it to the earth below. But now it's time to get that hike underway.

The Root
of the Matter

THE FOREST IS full of life, both life you can see and life you can't. For this reason, unless you are lost and have no choice but to go bushwhacking or are in an area you know well and know it's okay to do so, on most hikes it's best to stick to well-established trails. In fact, most national, provincial, and state parks insist that you do.

Sticking to trails is partly for your benefit. Off the trail, you can run into plants that are not friendly to hikers. Poison oaks and sumacs and poison ivies, found across the continent, make nutritious food for many animals, but they can give human hikers an extremely painful itch and rash. In the northeast, the arching roots of hobblebush can trip the unwary. In the forests of the Pacific Northwest, devil's club, which has particularly nasty thorns, abounds. You can keep yourself safe from all of these if you stay on the trails. Well-worn trails also put some welcome space between you and animals you'd rather not meet, such as snakes—unless they happen to be sunbathing in the open—or come into contact with, such as ticks. If you read on, I will tell you later about my own encounter with these unpleasant little creatures.

Sticking to trails also benefits the forest. Every person who walks around a mud puddle rather than through it increases the width of the trail, which can damage delicate vegetation, lead to erosion, and change drainage patterns in the forest. Creating trails can be a challenging process and popular ones are difficult to maintain if too many people stray from them. So, depending on the time of year, come prepared with footwear that allows you to splash through puddles and mud. (Any children you are traveling with will be more than happy to follow this advice.) If you must walk off the beaten track, you can "make like a herd of elk," as a hike leader once explained to Jane. That is, a group of hikers spreads out to minimize the impact of their footfalls.

And just one more thing before we head off. In places where invasive species pose a problem, use the boot cleaners at trail heads to brush hitchhiking seeds off your boots. The forest will thank you for your thoughtfulness.

YOU MAY THINK of roots mainly as obstacles to step over as you take your forest hike. When roots intrude onto the trail, you need to spend more time looking at the ground than the scenery around you. Roots become especially treacherous when they are wet or icy. Jane tells me that one day while she was hiking in her local forestlands, her foot landed on a long root hidden under leaves. As slippery as ice, the root stretched downhill away from the path. She almost ended up going down over the edge with it. I had a similar experience in my forest in Germany that I'll tell you about later. Both of us can attest that it is good to pay attention when there are roots around.

What can be an annoyance for us is, of course, vital for a tree. At the most basic level, roots anchor trees so they stand firm when their tops sway in the wind. Sometimes when the soil gets saturated, roots lose their hold on the ground and high winds blow the trees over. Trees are also prone to tipping over in places where there is not much soil for their roots to penetrate. If you come across a downed tree, you can get some idea of how far its supporting root system extends. For example, by a trail Jane walks on Chuckanut Mountain in Washington State, the root mass of a downed Douglas fir towers above hikers, completely dwarfing them.

Beyond the supporting roots, fine feeder roots feel their way through the upper layers of the forest floor searching for water and nutrients. In Philadelphia, the University of Pennsylvania's Morris Arboretum hosts a great visual demonstration of this. The distance a tree's roots travel is painted onto the asphalt path so you can see that even when you are walking way out beyond the spread of the tree's branches, you are still walking on its delicate root system—yet another reason for you to keep to trails in the forest. Trees don't appreciate you stepping on their toes.

The weight of one person might not seem like much, but over time repeated footfalls can compress the forest soil, making it difficult for the trees' roots to breathe. Does it sound odd to you that roots breathe? Like us, roots breathe oxygen and drink water. They can only do this when the soil contains sufficient open spaces to store air and water for the trees' feeder roots to find. By restricting footfalls to trails, you can minimize damage to the trees' root systems. Soil compaction, and the resulting loss of spaces for oxygen and water, was just one of the reasons having to use heavy machinery in my job as a forester caused me such distress. Compacted soils are not good for long-term forest health, and once soil has been compacted it takes hundreds, even thousands, of years of hard work by trees and all the tiny creatures working underground to reconstruct the open spaces that have been lost.

In some places in North America, notably the American South, trees such as baldcypress have root systems that spend a lot of time underwater. To get around the problem of submerged roots, baldcypress trees grow "knees." These specialized roots rise out of the ground around the main trunk. (Yet another hazard to the unwary hiker if these roots are growing right in the trail, which can happen.) Cypress knees can grow up to ten feet (three meters) tall, which is tall enough to extend above the average high-water line, and they are thought not only to stabilize the trees in their watery environment, but also to help the roots breathe by transporting oxygen from the air to the parts that are submerged, acting as a kind of snorkel—although that has yet to be proven.

But roots do more than act as physical support (or even as breathing tubes). You could say the essence of tree-ness lies in a tree's roots, for the roots are the first part of the tree to grow and the part that persists most reliably as trees age.

When a tree seed falls to the ground—a poplar seed drifting on the breeze in its coating of fluff, perhaps, or a seed dropped from a pinecone by a squirrel hastily eating its lunch—the first part to start growing is the root, stretching out to find water to fuel the seedling's growth.

The root is a constant as a tree grows. If the crown of a spruce gets toppled in a winter storm, the tree can grow a new one. Long-lived yew trees grow new trunks after disaster (say, lightning) strikes, which is one reason ancient yews often have multiple trunks. Old Tjikko, a Norway spruce growing in the Swedish province of Dalarna, is estimated to be 9,500 years old and is thought to be the oldest living tree in the world. It has shoots that are younger than this, but the root is its source of longevity. The roots of trees can survive for thousands of years, weathering changes in climate and storing centuries of experience.

Some forests that appear to be formed from multiple individual trees are actually a collection of shoots growing from a single massive root system. Aspens and poplars grow this way, which is why it is so difficult to remove individual trees from your property. When you cut down one shoot, another grows in its place. Pando, a forest of quaking aspen in Utah that spans 106 acres (43 hectares), is commonly classified as a single organism despite the vast area it covers and the numbers of shoots it contains.

If the forest or woodland you are exploring is growing on sandy soil and the trail has been trodden down or perhaps follows the bank of a fast-flowing stream, you might see exposed roots. Stop and look more closely. Can you see the roots of one tree entwined with the roots of the tree next to it? Scientists have discovered that the roots can fuse together, which is one way trees share resources amongst themselves. Trees know that each individual tree has a role to play in the overall health of the forest, so they will reach out and support each other to ensure that the forest, as a whole, stands strong.

As you walk along the trail, feel the surface beneath your feet. Are you walking over sandy soil or rocky soil? Are you rustling your way through dead leaves or does the needle-covered trail muffle sound, silently compressing under each step you take and then springing back up again after you have passed? It can be fascinating to watch the hiker in front of you to see how the forest floor reacts when their feet apply and then release pressure on the ground.

Each soil type you encounter suits different types of trees, and the trees that grow in the forest contribute to developing the soil they prefer. Take the red spruce forests that grow in the cool, moist heights of the Central Appalachians. The thick layer of discarded needles on the forest floor increases the acidity of the already acid sandstone soil. The acidic leaf litter decomposes slowly, and the red spruce trees cast shade. Nutrients are hard to come by, so the thrifty red spruces engineer an ecosystem that makes it difficult for other tree species to put down roots. These ecosystems then become home to animals that specialize in them—animals that sometimes know no other home and are so small that if their home is destroyed, they do not have the means to travel to find new ones.

As you watch where you put your feet, the number of roots on the surface can give you some clues about the forest you are walking through. At a low elevation, lots of roots can indicate a high water table. Just as your skin could not stay healthy if you sat in a bathtub all day long, trees—unless they are water specialists like baldcypress or tupelos—try to keep their feet as dry as possible so their roots don't rot from being underwater.

When you hike at higher elevations on rocky ground, you find roots at the surface because they don't have anywhere else to go. There is just not enough soil for them to bury themselves very deep. As you know from your high school science lessons, gravity pulls everything downhill. After a rain, water that doesn't soak into the ground flows downhill taking soil with it. The valleys fill with soil while the hilltops are washed bare. Trees can help slow this process, but only if a lot of them are growing together so their roots can hold the soil in place. This is one reason conifers dominate at higher elevations. Because they discard and replenish their needles gradually over a number of years, they are better equipped to grow in thin, less nutritious soils than trees that lose all their leaves at once and have to expend a lot of energy growing a whole set of new ones every year.

Once a forest has grown, the tangle of roots beneath a tree makes a fine place for animals, both small and large, to create their homes. If the root systems are large enough, bears may dig their winter dens under them. Wolves may dig their dens under the protection of smaller tree roots to keep their pups safe from bears. Foxes and coyotes are next in line. On an even smaller scale, rats, voles, and mice may dig extensive tunnels under the protection of tree roots. Tiny as they are, chipmunks can dig burrows up to thirty feet (nine meters) long. Check to see if you can find any holes under and around the roots of trees along the trail. What do you think might have made them?

Tree roots are the source of life not only for individual trees but also for plant life in general on this planet. If the forest you are walking in has large rocks, look to see how the tree roots are strong enough to create fissures in the rocks over time. Along with lichen (more on them later), early trees were important in building soil by breaking down rock into the mineral portion of soil. As trees grew and shed their leaves, they added organic matter. Micro-organisms soon moved in to help recycle nutrients. Trees, like most plants, use sunlight, carbon dioxide, and water to manufacture carbohydrates, almost, but not quite, conjuring food from thin air. All animals rely on plant food in some way, either by eating it directly or by eating other animals that have dined on plants. So, tree roots create the conditions for other plants to grow, providing the building blocks for life on Earth as we know it today.

~ 3 ~

What the Trees Can Tell You

WHEN I TRAINED as a forester, I was taught to value trees that grew tall and straight, for these were the ones that had the most economic value. When I started showing visitors around the forest I managed, the trees that drew their attention were those whose shape showed their character or whose trunks carried scars as a testament to all they had endured over the course of their long lives. Look up from the roots at your feet to the trunks around you. What might they tell you about the forest where you are walking?

You might think that the width and height of a tree would tell you something about how long the tree has been growing, but that's not necessarily the case. Many situations can cause trees to grow slowly. In an intact, ancient forest, huge trees shade the ground, using nearly all the sunlight that falls on their canopies to generate food to fuel their growth, while the younger trees wait patiently in the shadows below. This is good because slow growth means strong, dense wood that resists breakage, rot, and insect damage. When a mother tree falls, a jagged opening appears in the tree canopy and all the youngsters waiting below start

Tree roots, Algonquin Provincial Park, Ontario

sprinting toward the light. I say sprinting in relative terms because trees live life in the slow lane and it will take the teenage trees another hundred years or so to reach the canopy, where they can finally spread out and bask in the sunlight themselves.

In Algonquin Provincial Park in Ontario, Canada, tall, white pines were harvested in the late nineteenth century and yet if you hike Big Pines Trail today, you can still see enormous pines that were alive back then. How did they escape the loggers? Although these trees were the same age as the felled giants (about one hundred years old), they were much smaller than the trees the loggers cut down because

they were growing in their shade. After their larger rela-
tions were removed, the small pines grew rapidly into the
impressive trees you see along the trail today. Researchers
have taken core samples from their trunks. The spacing
of the annual rings clearly shows the accelerated pace of
growth after the area was logged in 1890. And so, what were
once stunted little trees finally had their day in the sun.

Tough conditions can also cause trees to grow slowly
for their entire lives. In an ancient forest of eastern white
cedar on the Niagara Escarpment in Ontario, Canada, the
trees are so small that it wasn't until the late 1980s that
anyone noticed they were hundreds of years old. The little
cedars cling to a rocky cliff, their roots penetrating narrow
cracks and their trunks growing into incredible shapes. One
is nicknamed The Snake because of the way the tree twists
and turns as it slithers down over the rockface. Another, on
a rock that must have shifted after the tree took hold, continues to grow even as it hangs upside down.

Look at the trunks around you. The giant redwoods of
the northern California coast have grown so tall that if you
stand in an old-growth grove, no matter how far back you
tilt your head, you can't possibly see their crowns. The tops
of the trees are so far off the forest floor that they catch fog
rolling off the ocean, which is how they get some of the
water they need to grow to such great heights. Their wide
bases flare out to give the trees the stability to reach heights
of three hundred feet (ninety meters) or more. Swampy
ground also calls for extra stabilization. In a place like Congaree National Park in South Carolina, you can see the flare
on the rounded bases of the tupelos as they rise out of the
water. If you look closely, you might even see a high-water
line. The top of the brown stain, where the moss stops growing, indicates the level of the latest flood.

Conifers such as spruce, pine, and fir usually grow up, straight as an arrow, often on slopes. If the ground moves beneath them, they may find themselves tilting sideways. When this happens, they adjust and realign their growth to vertical and their trunks bend in a distinct J-shaped curve. Sometimes you can use these curves as a handy place to sit and rest. Just don't do this when the tree is leaning out over a cliff. Jane once witnessed a mother lining her children up on such a tree for a photograph until the woman's teenaged son happened to mention that he was hanging out over a void.

Shifting ground is not the only reason tree trunks might develop a bend. In Harvard Forest, an ecological research area in Petersham, Massachusetts, a large white pine with a curved trunk is visible from the French Road Trail. The Great Hurricane of 1938 tipped it over. It survived the storm and as it continued to grow, the trunk reoriented to vertical, creating the bend at the bottom.

Then there is the curious case of trees that bend at a 90-degree angle before straightening out and growing toward the sky. In this case, something completely different has happened. At some stage in the tree's early growth, its top snapped off. Perhaps another tree fell on it in a storm. The tree's goal is to reach sunlight, but how can it grow tall when its top is missing? Ever resourceful, the tree turns one of its branches into a surrogate trunk. This involves an abrupt change in direction, and you see a sharp turn in what you thought was the tree's trunk but is, in fact, a repurposed branch. The tree now looks like a person who has stretched an arm out to one side and then raised one hand by bending the arm at the elbow. Hi, the tree seems to be saying, I'm still here. I'm just fine.

Disease or insects can also affect how trunks grow. White pines are iconic trees of northeastern forests. Weevils attack a number of conifers, including white pines, eating their growing tips when the trees are still young. Branches that have not yet become fixed in their sideways growth pattern switch to vertical and stretch upward to replace the lost leader. As the tree matures, it ends up with more than one trunk. Having multiple trunks, however, is not healthy for the pines. Sooner or later, one will snap off, leaving a gaping wound in the tree.

Multiple trunks can also be a sign of human activity in the forest. Hardwoods (trees with leaves rather than needles) are much more likely than conifers to sprout from the base after they have been cut down. Historically, people have profited from this by cutting back hardwoods so they grow a large number of thin trunks that can be harvested and used for poles and firewood. People in Europe still practice the art of "coppicing." If you come across hardwoods with multiple trunks and they are not shrubby trees that naturally grow this way, you could be seeing trees that have regrown from stumps after loggers felled the original trees.

Other strange shapes are formed by natural processes. These can be especially fun to spot and are good candidates for photographs to share with friends. For example, you might also find trunks that have perfectly formed holes in the center where the trunk started to grow, split in two, and then the two parts rejoined to create a single trunk again. Or trunks that fuse with the trunks of trees growing next to them. Sometimes called "marriage trees," these can certainly look as though the trees are giving each other a big kiss. Some of the redwoods in southern Oregon and northern California have protuberances jutting out from their lower trunks that look like giant droopy noses. These burls are formed in response to environmental stress or injury. They contain buds and if they grow all the way to the ground, the trees can use them to clone themselves if something happens to the parent tree.

Even when trunks grow mostly straight, the wood inside sometimes twists in a spiral. You can see this most clearly on standing dead pines that have lost their bark. The wood looks like a wrung-out towel. Scientists suggest wood fibers arranged in spiral patterns bend more easily in high winds. As the trees twist and turn, they can also rid themselves of a burden of snow. Humans can retreat inside when the weather turns bad, but trees have no choice but to stand where they are and stick it out. Spiral growth patterns can help them survive.

People have long exploited the wonderful shapes in which wood grows. Boat builders from antiquity to today have gone out into the woods to find trees with trunks and branches perfectly shaped for the keels and ribs of their vessels. A marvelous collection of tree crooks from live oak waits at Mystic Seaport in Connecticut to be milled into planks for the next big wooden boat restoration project.

Once you start looking, you will find the trees' growing history recorded in the twists and turns of their trunks. Despite detours and dead ends, trees are resilient and determined to find a way to continue growing as straight and tall as they can toward the light.

~ 4 ~

Leaves,
Nuts, and Seeds

TREES ARE MORE than just trunks, of course. They have branches, as well. The main role of a branch is to carry the leaves and needles trees use to make food and to support the structures trees use to grow the nuts and seeds they need to start a new generation.

Trees can use leaves to make food only when the sun hits them. Once the forest trees tower above their lower branches, shading their leaves, the trees stop keeping these branches alive and they eventually rot and drop off. Meanwhile, the tree grows wood to seal off the branch stub so infection doesn't enter the trunk.

Look at the lower part of a tree to see the scars left in the bark where a branch once grew. In trees with smooth bark, branch scars look like an eye with an eyebrow arched over it. Because trees expand in width all the way up but grow in height only from the top, no matter how tall a tree grows, as long as these branch scars are visible, they will forever remain the same distance from the ground. Therefore, if you nail a "welcome" sign to the tree at the end of your driveway, it will stay the same height to greet visitors for as long as the

Branch patterns (in white),
Bruce Peninsula National Park, Ontario

tree is there. Although, I think it would be a nice gesture to the tree if you were to use a post to support your sign instead.

When a tree is cut down and milled into lumber, the knots in the wood show where branches once grew. Foresters often cut off a tree's lower branches when they are still young, so the knots stay small. If you look for a fallen tree, you can examine the places where the branches protrude. Sometimes, after the softer fibers in the wood have weathered away, the branch stub coming out of the trunk sports a spiral pattern that makes it look as though the branch was screwed into the trunk instead of growing straight out of it.

You can also examine any cut trunks you find along the trail to see if you can find one where the saw sliced through the exact spot in a trunk where a branch grew. These are hard to find but fascinating to examine. You can see the branch as a light patch that interrupts the tree rings as it extends out from the center, a bit like a hand pointing to the time on a clockface. If the branch fell off while the tree was young, the tree will have had time to grow new wood completely over the scar. From the outside, there is no longer evidence a branch grew here. It is only when the tree is cut open in precisely the right place that you can see its remains.

Because leaf production is all about light, a tall tree, such as the white oak that grows in the East, favors smaller leaves at the top so at least some light falls onto the leaves growing on branches below. You might also notice that leaves growing closer to the ground, where the forest is shady, tend to be larger and softer. This is because trees are trying to absorb as much light as possible with these shaded leaves. Understory trees such as dogwoods live their lives in low light. They not only have larger leaves to absorb all the light they can get but also grow their branches in flat tiers so their leaves are spread out in single layers to make the most efficient use of the light that filters down to them.

There is another advantage to smaller leaves at lofty heights. The giant redwoods on the north California coast grow so tall that the base of the trees live in one kind of climate while the crown lives in another. Accordingly, the trees have different needles at different heights above the forest floor. The needles at the top are shorter and more tightly packed to reduce water loss because it is much windier at the top of the tree than at the bottom.

Deciduous trees discard their leaves once a year. Whereas we do spring cleaning, for most of these trees, it's all about fall clean up. They withdraw useful substances like chlorophyll from their leaves and break it down to reclaim the nitrogen it contains so they can reuse it the following year.

Removing chlorophyll, which is green, reveals the yellows and oranges that are in the leaves all the time. The trees then pump any waste products into their leaves and loosen the connection that holds the leaves onto the branches. This process also traps sugars in the leaves, and it is these sugars that turn the leaves that gorgeous red color we love so much. The loosened leaves eventually fall off in a stiff breeze. What for the trees is a mundane housekeeping chore provides us with a spectacular display of color that is most intense when there is a moist spring, a dry late summer, and a fall with sunny days and cool nights. In New England, where the displays are particularly vibrant, color peaks in late September to the north and at higher elevations, and in late October farther south.

The fall displays in Lost Maples State Natural Area near Vanderpool, Texas, rival those in New England, although they peak a little later, usually in November. It might seem strange to think of maples that far south, but the glaciers that covered the northern part of North America in the last ice age drove many tree species south, and the maples in this park are a remnant population that clung on in the park's moist canyons when the surrounding landscape warmed up. You can see similar islands of northern trees in the Chisos Mountains in Big Bend National Park along the Rio Grande in southern Texas, where Douglas fir and aspen grow.

Not all deciduous trees lose their leaves in fall. The live oak, a common tree in southeastern forests, holds onto its leaves through the winter, discarding them in spring as the new leaves start to form. Each live oak hears a different drummer, so while one may discard all its old leaves before its new leaves start to unfurl, another may wait so you barely notice a time when it is not green. Trees, like us, are individuals, and some have slightly different ways of doing things.

Although evergreen trees stay green year-round, this doesn't mean they never discard their leaves or needles, both of which get old and worn out. It's just that evergreen trees don't discard all their greenery at the same time, so most of the time we don't notice. Pines, for instance, keep their needles for two to five years, depending on the species. The frugal spruce can hold onto its short, stubby needles for five to seven years. Jane, a Washington State University Extension Master Gardener Volunteer Educator, says every year the plant clinic gets telephone calls from homeowners concerned that the western red cedars in the neighborhood are dying. Callers are relieved to hear that the clumps of brown foliage are part of a completely normal process of needle renewal and the trees are just fine.

Even more startling to some people are the larches that turn gold every year and drop every one of their needles. Surely, they must have died. But, no, once again, this is a natural process. Somewhere along its evolutionary path, this species of conifer simply chose to renew its needles every year like a deciduous tree. In Washington State, their golden fall colors contrast with the fiery reds of blueberry bushes, making late-season hikes on the east side of the North Cascades stunningly beautiful.

Much of the action in a forest may be happening way above your head. This is where the leaves are unfurling, the blossoms are opening, and the fruits are forming. You can't see up there, but you can find clues by looking at the ground. Check for leaves and needles on the sides of the trail. In a West Coast forest, you can probably find the huge leaves of the aptly named bigleaf maples. Often bigger than your head, the leaves are always a big hit with children.

As Jane camped her way around the country to research parts of this book, she would often sit outside at a picnic table under trees. She was amazed by how often twigs with leaves or needles attached would land around her, especially if a squirrel was bounding from branch to branch in search of pinecones, nuts, or acorns.

You'll probably find quite a lot of this forest debris on the ground as you hike along the trail. You can check the lengths of the pine needles and count the number in a bundle. Eastern white pine needles grow in bundles of five. Jack pine and red pine needles both grow two to a bundle. Red pine needles are long, up to six-and-a-half inches (over fifteen centimeters), while jack pine needles are much shorter. The singleleaf pinyon, found in the Southwest, is the only single-needle pine in the world, so if you find branches with single needles on them, and you're not standing near a singleleaf pinyon, the branches you have found do not come from any kind of pine. Spruce and fir have single, flattened needles attached directly to branches. Spruce needles will poke you. Fir needles will not. Douglas fir and hemlock needles attach to branches with a tiny stalk. White cedars, red cedars, and sequoias have scaly leaves instead of needles.

The cones on the forest floor can also tell you about the conifers towering over you. Remember, though, that the size of the cone tells you nothing about the mature size of the tree. Giant sequoias, the most massive trees in the world by volume, produce relatively tiny cones: only one-and-a-half to three inches (four to seven-and-a-half centimeters) long. The sugar pine, however, the tallest pine in the world, produces the longest cones in the world, measuring up to twenty-four inches (sixty centimeters).

We usually call all cones pinecones, even though all conifers produce cones. Indeed, that is the definition of the word conifer: a tree that produces cones. You probably have an image of a woody cone covered in hard scales that open to release the trees' seeds, but not all cones look like that. That small red thing on a yew that Jane always thought was a fruit is, in fact, a single seed dressed up in a striking red coating to encourage birds and animals to eat it and disperse it. This red, fleshy covering is a modified cone scale, making this "aril" a modified cone. Tempting though it looks, don't try eating it. The coating is edible, but the seed inside is poisonous. The poison does not harm the birds that eat these false fruits because the seeds pass through their systems intact, so they can then be deposited along with their own personal packet of fertilizer to start a life of their own far from the parent tree, thanks to the bird's air mail service.

You can find a variety of nuts on the forest floor, some of which you can eat but most of which you should leave to the chipmunks, deer, and black bear, or birds such as jays and ruffed grouse. These include beechnuts and hickory nuts, walnuts and butternuts, pecans, and chestnuts. Wild turkeys eat just about anything in the open forests they frequent throughout North America, including nuts. They swallow grit and pebbles so they can break the nuts down in their muscular gizzards. According to ornithologist and author John K. Terres, it takes a wild turkey about an hour to crush pecans, shell and all.

Acorn woodpeckers in oak forests peck holes in standing dead trees and stuff an acorn into each hole as though they were stuffing a bun with cherries. The acorns fit so tightly into their individual holes that other animals cannot remove them. When the acorns shrink as they dry out, the woodpeckers move them to smaller holes to keep them safely tucked away so they'll have something to eat in winter. Generations of woodpeckers may use the same dead tree until it is riddled with holes. The birds prefer forests with a mix of oak species to ensure their acorn supply. That way, if one species doesn't produce acorns for some reason, the woodpeckers can scavenge from others.

Pinecones and nuts are heavy, and don't travel far unless birds and animals carry them off. Oak trees have done a great job co-opting squirrels and woodpeckers to transport their seeds, but some trees prefer to trust their luck to the wind. Maples, for instance, tuck their seeds into those single- or double-bladed helicopter rotors that twirl down when the wind blows. The seeds weigh more than the rotors, so the seed packages land with the seed pointed down, giving the seeds a better chance of taking root where they come to rest. Silver and red maples drop their whirligigs in late spring, while sugar maples abandon theirs to the breeze in the fall. Poplars and willows have tiny seeds coated in fluff that accumulate to form an airy carpet on the forest floor.

The Beauty of Bark

LOOKING AT TRUNKS and branches inevitably leads to looking at their protective covering: bark. Bark is to trees as skin is to people, a waterproof layer that contains and protects delicate internal organs. Just as dead skin cells drop off people as they grow and new skin forms, dead bark drops off trees and new bark forms. And trees, like people, tend to get wrinkles as they age.

Some trees, like some people, develop a tougher skin than others. This is partly related to family genetics. For instance, pitch pines, which have adapted to grow in places where wildfires are frequent, develop thick insulating bark at an early age, while American beech trees keep their youthful complexions for most of their lives. The American beech originated in tropical climates where wildfires are rare. Knowing their hosts will likely live long, fire-free lives, lots of plants and other living organisms attach themselves to trees living in tropical places to get a leg up toward the light. These hangers-on are not in themselves harmful, but if a large number gather in one place, their weight can overwhelm a tree. Smooth bark offers few places for them to gain

Birch bark, Jacques Cartier National Park, Quebec

purchase, hence the beeches' wrinkle-free look. So, thanks to the trees' different genetic legacies, one has thick, craggy skin and the other looks forever young. Between these two extremes, bark comes in what seems like an infinite variety of patterns and shapes, from the smooth bark on lean, muscular-looking hornbeams to hickories so shaggy that bats can shelter under their hanging strips of bark.

Not only does tree bark become more textured as trees age (even those smooth-skinned beeches), but you also sometimes see a mixture of smooth and wrinkled bark on a single tree. The lower trunk and bark can have wrinkles, while the new growth still sports a youthful look. And, just like your skin, on any individual tree, the bark can look more weather-beaten in some spots than others. In northern latitudes, wet snow can freeze and thaw between bark ridges, causing the bark to have more wrinkles on the side of the tree that accumulates snow. It's a bit like wrinkles forming around the eyes of people who have to squint against the sun a lot. The weather the skin is exposed to shapes the contours of the skin itself.

Most trees have a greenish inner bark. This is usually covered up by thick bark ridges and wrinkles, but if the outer bark is thin and relatively smooth, light can get through and the tree can use this green inner bark for photosynthesis. This might seem strange to you. It's the leaves that photosynthesize, right? But the green pigment is the same chlorophyll that tree leaves use to turn sunlight, carbon dioxide, and water into food, and it works in bark, too.

Bark photosynthesis gives an energy boost to trees that grow in challenging conditions. Striped maples, for example, make their home in the shady understory of northeastern woods, and you can clearly see the stripes of green in their bark. They take advantage of the more open canopy in a hardwood forest to do some bark photosynthesis when the other trees are taking their winter break. Aspens, which grow in the same nutrient-poor conditions as many conifers, use the chlorophyll in their bark to keep some photosynthesis going even after they have shed their leaves in fall. Once their new spring foliage shades their bark, they rely once again on their leaves to produce food.

Bark is a great way to identify trees after they have dropped their leaves in winter or when they grow so tall that their branches and needles rise way up over your head. Birch trees have papery peeling bark, which Jane discovered burns well even when wet. And the smooth bark of balsam fir is covered with resin-filled blisters. Jane punctured a blister with her thumbnail and discovered the resin was really, really sticky and hard to remove. Tiny green needles grow from the bark of pitch pine, ready to sprout into new branches should the old ones be destroyed by fire. Sycamore bark peels off in patches, which makes the tree particularly well suited to urban settings. When pollution clogs the bark's breathing pores, the tree just sloughs off its outer layer and grows a new skin. Jane was particularly taken with the knobby lumps on the bark of Hercules' club, a tree that grows in the South. It is also known as toothache tree or tingle tongue because if you chew the leaves, bark, or twigs, your mouth goes numb, which helps if you have toothache. That said, the bark can cause skin irritation, vomiting, and diarrhea, so it might be better to find a different toothache remedy.

One way of narrowing down what tree you're looking at is to examine the small openings all over the bark through which the trunk breathes. These tiny, mouth-shaped openings can be linear, diamond-shaped, oval, or round. They are easiest to see on trees with smooth bark, and they show up particularly well on the dark, slightly shiny bark of young cherries. The tree uses chlorophyll to manufacture sugars from carbon dioxide, sunlight, and water. As it does so, it releases oxygen into the air as a byproduct of photosynthesis. At the same time, trees are respiring—that is to say, taking in oxygen and exhaling carbon dioxide. Think of photosynthesis as step 1 in a tree's feeding process. It manufactures sugars but, like us, the tree must then combine these sugars with oxygen to generate the energy it needs to grow, and, just as we do, the tree gets this oxygen by inhaling it.

It then releases carbon dioxide as a waste product. Don't worry, though, this doesn't mean trees are pumping out carbon dioxide and not oxygen after all. Whenever a tree is photosynthesizing, it pumps more oxygen into the air than carbon dioxide.

Identifying trees by their bark requires a good guide-book and a sharp eye but even if you don't plan to use bark for tree identification, it is fascinating to check out all the patterns. If you have children with you, take along a piece of paper and crayons and make rubbings of the different textures you find. The nature writer and conservationist known as Grey Owl, who worked for Canada's Dominion Parks Branch in the 1930s, once described forests as cathedrals. In the cathedrals of Europe, people often make rubbings of the brass effigies marking the tombs of medieval knights. If you have the good luck to go walking in an old-growth forest, you can make rubbings of the bark of trees that started growing while these knights were still on the battlefield.

Just as we get scars on our skin, trees get scars on their bark and they have stories to tell. Some tree scars come from physical injury. You might notice a tree with an inverted V-shaped scar at the base of its trunk. A common cause for this type of scar is fire. If fire burns hot enough, it damages the living layer of wood just under the bark. When the bark falls off, it leaves a triangular gap, wider at the bottom where the fire burned hotter, and narrower at the top where there were fewer flames. As the wind whips fire along the ground, the flames burn hottest and longest on the side of the tree protected from the wind. The "church door" or "cat face," as foresters sometimes call it, is always on the side of the tree downwind of the fire. Injuries inflicted when loggers pulled trees from forests can result in similar-shaped scars at the base of trees. Knowing a bit of the forest's history can help you pinpoint the cause of the damage.

If you look higher up the trunk, you might find another scar, a long, narrow split caused by lightning. Sometimes lightning strikes so deep, the opening allows fungi to enter and start rotting the tree from the inside. Jane came across an example of this on a magnificent white pine in Algonquin Provincial Park. There were small tan-colored mushrooms growing all around the long vertical gash. It's only a matter of time before this tree will succumb to the fungus and die. Luckily, trees die as slowly as they live, so it will be quite some time before this giant falls.

Frost ribs provide further evidence of the extremes of weather trees endure. These ribs form when the low-angled winter sun strikes the tree's trunk and warms it. When night falls, the bark loses its heat and contracts more quickly than the underlying wood. After a few of these warming and cooling cycles, the bark splits. Come spring, the tree grows new bark along the length of the split. The new growth protrudes slightly from the old, and the new bark, like the scar tissue people grow, has a different texture. Trees get similar injuries in times of drought, a bit like when you get a crack in your lip. I don't know if these cracks cause pain for the tree, but I do know that a crack in the delicate skin of your lip is not at all pleasant.

Trees can also carry scars caused by infections, like pock marks after a severe case of chicken pox. You can see small, sunken circles in the smooth bark of American beech that have been attacked by fungi. If the pock marks don't go all the way around the tree, it still has enough intact vessels under its bark to transport the food and water it needs to survive. The scars show that despite the infection, the tree is putting up a good fight.

There are infections and then there are invaders. Large pieces of bark lying on the forest floor can tell you whether beetles have been munching on the trees. Hold a section of bark up to the light to see if you can spot the holes where the beetles exited as they chewed their way out of their larval nurseries. If you look on the underside of the bark—the part that would have been attached to the tree—you might see evidence of the galleries the larvae excavated as they ate their way through the living layer of dividing cells just beneath the bark. You can trace the larvae's wandering paths because the galleries grow wider as the larvae grow fatter. The dotted line of small, neat holes circling a trunk are the work of a medium-sized woodpecker called a sapsucker, but we will talk more about woodpeckers and their role in the forest later in the book.

One place where you can see bark damage clearly, and sometimes as a fight to the death, is when vines with tiny rootlets, such as ivy, attach themselves to the tree's bark. These vines can weaken and eventually kill trees by preventing light from reaching the leaves, as well as by their sheer weight. Twining vines like honeysuckle wrap themselves around trunks in their quest to reach the light. If the vine does not wrap around the tree too tightly, it imprints a spiral track in the tree's bark and you can clearly see where it grew long after it has died and fallen off. If it wraps itself more tightly, the whole trunk grows in a twisted spiral. Tighter still, and the vine strangles the tree it was using as support, causing its demise. In some cases, the tree fights back, asserting its dominance by growing bark over the offending invader and covering the vine completely. This, too, leaves a telltale scar, sometimes in the shape of a smile, making the tree look particularly satisfied in its moment of victory. Jane exchanged a friendly greeting with just such a tree in Congaree National Park in South Carolina.

~ 6 ~

Hitching a Ride or Paying the Rent?

THE TREES IN the forest support and protect an amazing number of life forms. Many use the trees' branches as ladders to climb closer to the light. A few are parasitic. Mistletoe comes to mind. Dwarf mistletoe in the forests of the Pacific Northwest penetrates a tree's branches to suck the life-giving sap out of its host. The mature plant then shoots seeds up to forty feet (twelve meters) through the air to progress through the canopy. Other branch riders are less selfish, and forests would not survive without them. So, let's look up to see which organisms are freeloading on the trees' hospitality and which are paying guests.

In the Pacific Northwest, a thread-like lichen called old man's beard drapes ancient trees. Lichens grow on trees and rocks in the forest, but have you ever seen them on buildings in a city? Probably not. This has nothing to do with the efficiency of the city clean-up crews and everything to do with the air quality downtown. If you find crusty lichens

Spanish moss, Okefenokee National Wildlife Refuge, Georgia

growing on the apple trees in your yard, be happy. They do not harm the tree but serve as a sign of low pollution levels in the air around your house. Branches festooned with old man's beard indicate that the forest is healthy.

Like all lichens, old man's beard is a partnership between fungi and one or more algae that combine to create a distinct organism. The fungi provide structural support and the algae photosynthesize to provide food. This is an efficient division of household duties: one partner puts a roof over their heads and the other puts food on the table. If you pick up a handful of old man's beard from the forest floor (you'll find a lot of it on the ground after winter storms), you'll discover that the long fungal thread down the middle is stretchy, which, for some reason, Jane finds incredibly entertaining. Perhaps if you spend a lot of time in the forest, you simply slow down and get amused by simple things. If you're walking with children—or even if you're not—you can try this for yourself. If the old man's beard is grayish in color, it has dried out and is waiting for the next rain to freshen it up. The color will brighten as the outer layer of fungus becomes wet and transparent, revealing the blues and greens of the algae inside. Time for them to get going and start making food! Lichens are just one of several amazing life forms that can survive long periods of desiccation with no apparent adverse effects. Scientists are currently researching how they do this.

Lichens come in a wide range of shapes, sizes, and colors, and with an intriguing array of names: fairy barf, pixie cup, gritty British soldiers, lipstick powderhorn. Some look like lettuce leaves or ruffles of icing on a cake. Others sport tiny cups on stalks or form colorful crusts on rocks. The silvers and yellows of rock lichen act as sunscreen to protect these exposed lichen as they, like trees, begin their excruciatingly slow task of breaking down rock to create the mineral components of soil. Lichens can be so delicate and lovely that people even make jewelry out of them, and they have long been used to make plant dyes. I would caution you, however, to leave them be. They grow extremely slowly, and they have important jobs to do in the forest.

Mammals large and small eat lichen: deer, flying squirrels, bats. Reindeer moss, which is actually a kind of lichen, is indeed eaten by reindeer (AKA caribou in North America). Slugs, beetles, and even some spiders graze on lichen. Lichen also provides comfort and protection. Diminutive hummingbirds and tiny northern flying squirrels use lichen to line their nests, and certain moths with lichen-patterned wings sleep on tree trunks during the day, hidden from the prying eyes of birds.

The trees in ancient forests in the Pacific Northwest rely on a leafy-looking lichen for the nitrogen essential to plant growth. Nitrogen abounds in the air but plants cannot take it up until it has been processed into a water-soluble form, which is what the blue-green algae in these lichens do. The towering giants wait for bacteria grazing on the lichen to get washed to the ground by rain or for the lichen itself to fall to the forest floor, where the decomposition process begins, releasing the nitrogen and making it available to the trees through their roots.

Early in the life of a Pacific Northwest forest, perhaps after a storm plows through or after a fire, pioneering trees such as red alder act as the principal nitrogen processors. Alders have special nitrogen-fixing bacteria in nodules on their roots that process atmospheric nitrogen into plant-available nitrogen. The alders' death and decay free up the nitrogen for the rest of the forest to use. After alders die, giant conifers start to grow and after about 150 years, when the nutrients left by the alders are all used up, the leafy-looking lichens take over the alders' fertilizing duties.

Something that looks much like old man's beard grows in southern forests. It's called Spanish moss, even though it's not Spanish and it's not a moss. It isn't a lichen, either. An air plant, it's related to the pineapple, except unlike pineapples, which grow on the ground, Spanish moss grows on trees. Early settlers harvested Spanish moss and processed it down to its fibers to create a rather uncomfortable stuffing for mattresses. Like old man's beard, Spanish moss is just hitching a ride. It doesn't harm the tree unless there's so much that the weight causes branches to snap.

Spanish moss plants are tiny. The hanging masses you see are made up of thousands of individual plants attached to one another to create a pale green, dangling fringe. There are, however, other individually larger and more colorful air plants in southern forests. The cardinal air plant, common in Big Cypress National Preserve west of Miami, Florida, has red bracts (modified leaves) that grow up to three feet (one meter) long. It can live for up to twenty years. At the end of its life, this air plant produces a single flowering spike and then dies.

Within the forest ecosystem, air plants create their own mini ecosystems. Their leaves funnel rainwater into tiny reservoirs, where the pooled water attracts insects. The insects attract frogs, which lay their eggs in the water. Lizards and snakes come to drink the water and eat the frogs' eggs. Red-shouldered hawks fly in to pick off the lizards and snakes. The air plants, which usually get their food from particles floating in the air, enjoy a more varied diet as frogs' eggs and insects in their reservoirs die and decay.

Ferns using trees to hitch a ride to the sun can also create new ecosystems far from the forest floor. Leather-leaf ferns in California's giant redwood forests can trap such vast quantities of organic debris in the crotches of the trees' branches that layers of soil form up to three feet (one meter) thick. The seeds of other trees, ranging from huckleberries to Douglas firs, land on the soil and take root, and there are animals living in these sky gardens whose feet never touch the ground. None of this amazing world can be viewed from below, but once you know it's there, you can start to imagine the riot of life playing out a couple of hundred feet above your head.

Live oaks in southern forests are covered with a fascinating plant called the resurrection fern. Capable of drying up and then springing back to life after it rains, resurrection ferns can lose up to 97 percent of their water content and lie dormant for up to a century. Add them to the list of organisms that scientists are busy researching to see how they manage the mysterious feat of desiccation and rebirth.

On the subject of regeneration, another organism found on trees has shown an even more impressive ability to hang on to life. In 1984, researchers in Antarctica dug out moss that had been frozen in the permafrost for more than fifteen hundred years. Within a few weeks, they had it growing in the lab. Mosses come with tiny but equally robust organisms that live within them. Tardigrades, commonly known as water bears or moss piglets, measure less than three-tenths of an inch (1 millimeter) and are truly amazing creatures. When a tardigrade starts to dry out, which it does when the moss it's living on gets dehydrated, it draws its tiny legs up into its body and curls up. From that point on it's virtually indestructible. Its small body withstands extremes of both cold and heat without suffering any damage. As soon as the temperature rises to comfortable levels and it's moistened by a drop of water falling on it, its legs pop back out and it begins to move as though it had never been temporarily immobilized. Tardigrades can even survive a short trip out into space unscathed.

Mosses and their hitchhikers may have superpowers of survival once they become established, but that doesn't mean it's easy for them to get a start on life. If you see a tree covered in moss in the Pacific Northwest, it's likely a vine maple or bigleaf maple. The notches in the bark of baby maples are just the right size for moss to get a foothold and the uneven bark traps water, creating a moist niche for moss to grow. Moss has a more difficult time attaching on larger trees, so the moss you see on the trunk is likely almost as old as the tree on which it's growing. This makes it especially disruptive to strip older trees of their moss: the tree has grown, conditions have changed, and the moss will not grow back.

If you examine mosses up close, some look like miniature forests growing below the larger forest towering over them. Mosses can't compete with trees for sunlight and they don't even try. As tiny as the trees are tall, they absorb the scraps of light that filter down through the canopy. In places where they might drown in the sea of leaves discarded by trees if they tried to grow directly on the forest floor, they seek higher ground. Logs that form islands above the debris, boulders dropped by passing glaciers, the bark of living trees in places where the wind doesn't blow and where water gathers in morning mists and after rain. They attach to whatever surface they are growing on with fragile filaments. If you walk gently over cushions of moss on rocks, pressing your feet straight down, they will do fine, but if you shuffle your feet as you walk, you will detach them from the structures that support them and the parts you have dislodged will die.

Tree bark sheds water, but mosses have no protective outer layer and absorb water directly, like a sponge. They are designed to grow in dense cushions that hold onto any water that falls on them. They don't need water to survive—they can exist in a dried-out dormant state for a long time—but they do need moisture if they are to photosynthesize and grow. A film of water on their surface also gives them the option of reproducing sexually. Moss sperm surf the wave of liquid on the moss's surface in their quest to find eggs to fertilize. When the weather is dry and the sperm lose their watery highway, mosses release spores instead of sperm. Mosses can also regenerate by cloning. They have a strategy for every eventuality, it seems. A moss in a Hawaiian forest has been cloning itself for fifty thousand years, making it one of the oldest multicellular organisms on Earth.

Mosses take nothing from the tree they grow on, but like all good tenants, they pay rent on the space they occupy. Mosses on trunks provide trees with a steady supply of moisture. The moss coating on the forest floor also fosters the growth of fungal threads that are vital to the trees' health. (But more on those threads later.)

Mosses are adept at squeezing the last drop of moisture from their surroundings. In winter, mosses growing on sunny rocks get moisture when the sun melts their coating of frost. At other times of the year, when the air cools and the surface they are growing on warms, dew forms and the thick mossy cushions immediately absorb the water droplets. If you see crunchy brown mosses in summer, don't worry. In the absence of moisture, they cannot manufacture the sugars they need to grow, but they are not dead. Just sleeping. Dried-up moss will soon rehydrate when the rains return, and it will be none the worse for wear.

~ 7 ~

The Importance
of Decay

YOU MIGHT THINK when you walk through the forest that someone really should come through and clean things up, but Nature doesn't work that way. What we see as a mess are the essential ingredients in the forest's grand recycling operation.

Let's start with standing dead trees, AKA snags. You might find them unsightly with their broken tops and bark falling off. What use could they be? It is true that without their leaves, they can no longer process sunlight or provide much shade or intercept raindrops to stop them from pounding directly onto the forest soil and compacting it or washing it away, but that does not make them a less integral part of the forest ecosystem.

Snags are apartment buildings for the forest's maintenance crew: for insects that break down wood for the next tier of forest recyclers, for birds and bats that eat the insects that attack living trees, and for small mammals that distribute seeds so the next generation of trees can grow. Snags provide a cafeteria, an observation platform, and an attention-grabbing space from which to broadcast important announcements. Not a bad place to snag yourself some living space.

The heavy hitters breach the snags first: pileated woodpeckers with strategically placed tufts of feathers to keep wood dust out of their nostrils as they vigorously hack away to create nesting cavities. When the wood in the snags gets softer over time, chickadees and white-breasted nuthatches excavate more modest dwellings. The fastidious nuthatch sweeps its cavity with a crushed insect as a chemical deterrent against pests. A great-crested flycatcher may hang a snakeskin by the front door of its snag cavity to signal this spot is taken. A downy woodpecker may surround the entrance with fungus or lichen to hide it from view. Eastern screech owls, which move in after the woodpeckers have moved on, bring blind snakes (reptiles that look a bit like large earthworms) into the cavity to feed their nestlings. If the owls don't gobble the snakes down for dinner, the snakes make themselves useful by eating insects that might compromise the health of the brood.

Woodpeckers like to build, use a cavity for a year, and then find a new place. Once the real estate developers move on, the tenants move in, specialists all. Owls and kestrels keep the forest's rodent population in check. Tree swallows and bluebirds catch insects on the wing, switching off with bats who take over the insect patrol at night. Tiny wrens chase beetles across the forest floor. And then the stunningly beautiful wood ducks arrive (although they prefer natural cavities if they can find them). Birds are not the only forest dwellers that use tree cavities. Squirrels, pine martens, raccoons, and porcupines all stay on the lookout for a dry, well-insulated spot to call home.

Bald eagles use tall, isolated snags as daytime perches that offer them unobstructed views of their surroundings. Kingfishers like to use snags next to waterways as convenient spots from which to launch aerial attacks on fish

Barred owlet, Silver Springs State Park, Florida

swimming below. Songbirds use them as places from which to belt out their messages of territorial conquest.

The next time you see a hole in a tree trunk, whether a natural cavity or one pecked out by a bird, stop a moment to see if it is occupied. Jane is no birder (just as she is not an entomologist), but she does know to pay attention when other people have stopped to look. And so one day at Silver Springs State Park in Florida, she also stopped to look at what at first glance appeared to be plain gray tree trunk, only to see the most enchanting barred owlet peeking out of a cavity. You just never know who is keeping a watchful eye on the hikers below.

Snags are chock full of insects. Black bears, with impressive strength and a no-nonsense focus on food, peel huge chunks of bark off snags to reveal the insects below, then push the dead trees over and shred the rotten wood to get at the insects inside.

Where you have dead trees, you also find stumps. If you have read *The Hidden Life of Trees,* you will know that it was an old stump that inspired me to embark on my journey of discovery into the secrets of forests. I came across what I thought was a circle of mossy stones only to discover that the rounded humps were in fact the remains of an ancient stump kept alive thanks to the nutrients pumped to it by the surrounding trees: an elder unable to feed itself but revered and cared for by generations of trees joined by community.

If you come across a stump on your forest hike, it's easy to tell if it is still alive or if it is dead. Just look to see how tightly the bark is attached. If the bark flakes off easily, then the stump is dead and already started on its long journey of decomposition. If the bark still adheres tightly to the wood below and is growing over the top of the stump, its fellow trees may well be keeping it alive.

Stumps of trees that have been cut down give you the opportunity to count tree rings. A tree grows a new ring of wood each year around its center. The width of the ring depends on how much the tree grows. Examining tree rings can tell scientists a lot about climate conditions such as snowpack, rainfall, and temperature, the frequency of fire, and even the level of cosmic rays, going back hundreds of years.

Tree-ring scientists gather data by drilling out slim core samples that go right to the center of the tree. Using this method, researchers from the Tree-Ring Laboratory at the University of Arkansas recently discovered a 2,624-year-old baldcypress in North Carolina, at the time of writing the oldest known wetland tree in the world. I'm not suggesting you go out into the forest armed with a drill, but if you come across the stump of a tree that has been cut down, which is very common alongside trails, you can have some fun examining the rings to see how uniform they are and, if you have the patience, perhaps even counting them to see how old the tree was when it was cut down.

How the stump is rotting can give you a clue as to whether it came from a conifer or a deciduous tree. Conifers, especially pines, accumulate resin in their interior wood. When this resin dries out, it makes the wood resistant to rot and so conifer stumps often decay more slowly than the stumps of hardwood trees. The resin-rich interior wood of dead pines was once a prized commodity. When burned, heavy pine tar could be extracted, and the steam produced during this process could be condensed into turpentine. Pine tar is used as a wood preservative and sealant for boats. Turpentine is used as a varnish and, when mixed with bees' wax, makes a high-grade furniture polish.

People also used to extract resin for making pine tar and turpentine from living trees. There is a forest walk around a pond in the Goethe State Forest near Tallahassee, Florida, where you can see grooves carved into longleaf pine trees from which dripping resin was directed into clay pots attached to the trunks. The only slight problem with this particular walk, as far as Jane was concerned, was the large number of alligators hanging out around the edge of the pond. It was alligator mating season and she could hear alligators advertising their desire from every direction. Alligators don't have vocal cords. They make these sounds by sucking air into their lungs and blowing it out in low-frequency sonic booms that make the water around them dance. Judging from the range in the pitch of the booms, some of the alligators in the forest that day were quite large.

No matter what kind of tree a stump came from, resinous or not, its rotting wood stores moisture. Over time, soil accumulates in the stump's cracks and crannies. This island of rotting wood provides a great nursery for seeds that cannot get a good start in the deep debris littering the forest floor. You might find ferns growing in old stumps or perhaps young huckleberry bushes. Sometimes you even find new trees, whose roots work their way down the outside of the stump, making it look as though the tree is growing on stilts. Over time, the stilts thicken, and the base of the tree loses its distinctive shape. In Algonquin Provincial Park in Canada, it is difficult for yellow birch to get started in the thick leaf litter the sugar maples leave on the forest floor. The sugar maples need this thick litter for their germination, but often the only chance yellow birch have of sprouting is when their seeds land on an old stump.

In swampy areas, when the stump rots from under the roots of the tree, using it to get a leg up on life, the gap between the trunk and the ground fills with forest debris, forming a hummock that keeps the tree roots up out of the water. There is not much oxygen in the sluggish water of swamps and the processes of decay are slow, resulting in dark brown or even black water as the tannins leaching out of surrounding trees accumulate. People in cities spend thousands of dollars on decorative ponds filled with black reflective water. If you take a hike out into forests in the South, you can see the marvelously reflective qualities of black water for free.

Speaking of water, dead and dying trees are important for many aquatic animals in the forest. Logs provide places for turtles to haul out and bask. Logjams created by woody debris form cool, shaded pools where young fish can grow protected from predators. Northern spring salamanders lay eggs under logs and twigs firmly anchored in flowing water, and gray tree frogs attach their eggs to vegetation in shallow water in ponds or swamps. (Interestingly, these little nocturnal frogs can survive being frozen for short periods of time during winter. Their organs shut down and they stop breathing, waiting for spring, when they thaw out and resume their amphibian lives.)

The small creatures making themselves at home in ponds and streams will tell you something about water quality in the forest. Take stoneflies, for example. These insects spend most of their lives (about a year) in streams before they crawl out onto dry land, slough off their skin to emerge as adults, and fly around for a few days. Then they mate, lay their eggs, and die. The larvae, known as nymphs, spend their time crawling around on the streambed. A good place to search for them is under stones. If you turn over a stone and see, attached to its underside, a flat, gray-brown creature with three pairs of legs and two long thread-like appendages projecting from its rear end, lift the stone out of the water to examine the creature up close. Stonefly nymphs need well-oxygenated water to survive, which means a swift-flowing stream. Finding them is a good indication that the stream they are living in is clean.

In many forests across North America, you may come across beaver ponds with well-maintained dams (which mean the beaver are still there) or ponds that are gradually diminishing in size as water seeps out through the dam (which means the beavers have moved on). Beavers depend on aspen, alder, and other trees around their lodges for food and when they have eaten their way through the supplies in one area, they leave and build a new lodge and dam where they can find more trees to feed on.

Skilled engineers, beavers are second only to humans in their ability to manipulate the habitats in which they live. Look at the next beaver dam you find. Which way are the twigs and branches facing? Jane took the test to see how she would construct a dam and decided she would lay the branches from side to side across the stream. Beavers are savvier construction engineers than Jane. They lay the branches angled up in the direction of the stream flow, so they catch mud and debris as the water flows over them. That way, the dam grows larger and stronger as the debris accumulates. Super-sensitive to flowing water, beavers rush to fix leaks. Interestingly enough, it's not the sight of the leak that triggers their behavior but the sound it makes. Given the choice between fixing a silent leak they can see and a speaker playing a recorded sound of running water, beavers will choose to plug holes around the speaker every time, even though no water is present.

Unless beavers have been busy, stumps in our forests today are usually the remains of trees that have been cut down. When trees fall of their own accord, they either snap off partway up the trunk, leaving a snag, or whole trees tumble over, ripping their supporting roots out of the ground. It can take a long time for the soil clinging to the roots of a large, uprooted tree to drop off. There will be a pit where the tree used to stand, and as the soil falls, it creates a mound. The forest floor then begins to take on the appearance of a lumpy, unmade bed. If you stand on the mound and look out over the pit, you will be looking in the direction the tree-toppling wind came from. If you look around, you might see other mounds and pits. If a big storm came through and toppled the trees all at the same time, the mounds and pits will be lined up in the same direction.

The pits often fill with water in the spring and provide temporary ponds where frogs and salamanders can lay their eggs, safe from the mouths of hungry fish. The fresh new soil in these pits and on the mounds makes a good spot for tree seeds to take root, a rare opportunity in a forest where a thick layer of debris covers most of the ground. The root mass provides a great place for animals such as chipmunks and river otters to dig dens in the soft soil. Pits and their accompanying mounds can last for five hundred to one thousand years, a sure sign the forest you are walking through is ancient and undisturbed.

Other forms of undulations on the ground are the long mounds created as the trunks of fallen trees decay. Once trees have fallen on the ground and their trunks begin to rot, we call them nurse logs because of their importance in regenerating life in the forest. They usually lie in a jumble of directions depending on where the wind was coming from on the day the individual trees fell.

Nurse logs are often covered in thick carpets of moss. Both moss and dead wood absorb moisture. So, in addition to serving as the first step in the forest's recycling system, they form part of the forest's climate control system. They are to the forest floor what a wet towel is to your neck if you wrap it around you on a hot day: a welcome antidote to the heat. Some of these logs contain so much water that they remain wet even after a fire has raged through the forest.

Nurse logs also often sport an impressive array of bracket

or shelf fungi. Some are as thick and sturdy as dinner plates. Others are as thin and delicate as butterfly wings. The fungi give you a clue as to whether they started to grow on the tree before or after it fell. Fungi reproduce by spores and for spores to travel on the breeze, they need to be dry. Therefore, bracket fungi always grow horizontally to the ground so that the "roof" of their fruiting bodies keeps the spores below from getting wet when it rains. If the bracket fungi are growing oriented vertically to the ground, they started life when the tree stood upright. If they are growing parallel to the ground, they started growing after the tree had fallen to the ground.

Nurse logs can be co-opted by animals for their own purposes. If you hear a weird whirring, thrumming sound in a northern forest, you may well be hearing a male ruffed grouse protecting his territory. He prefers a downed log with vegetation around it so he can sneak on and off without being seen. He also prefers a log of large diameter so that his drumming spot is up high, and he gets a good view of his surroundings. He chooses his log with care because he will use it again and again, always drumming in the same spot, facing in the same direction. He starts by moving his wings back and forth slowly, then faster and faster, sounding a bit like a small engine turning over before it finally catches. An old mossy log will show signs of wear at the spot where the grouse has chosen to broadcast his message through the forest.

It can take hundreds of years for nurse logs to disappear completely. In 1890, loggers in Algonquin cut down a mighty white pine but must have found some defect in the wood, for they abandoned some of the trunk. It lies there still, over a century later, slowly returning nutrients to the soil.

~ 8 ~

Spotlight
on the
Decomposers

IN AN URBAN SETTING, we think of earthworms as star decomposers and recyclers of material. They play an important role in North American forests, but only in those forests not buried in the last ice age by the glaciers that covered Canada, the area around the Great Lakes, and most of New England. When the ice retreated ten to twelve thousand years ago, earthworms had been eliminated and other decomposers, such as slugs, snails, and millipedes, moved in to take their place. The forests adapted to their new maintenance crew and today earthworms are considered invasive in these forests because their decomposition schedules move too quickly for these slower-paced forests to handle.

Earthworms, however, are hard at work in forests farther south. When rain falls in forests beyond the glaciers' icy reach, it not only infiltrates pores in the soil but also flows into drainpipes. I'm not talking about drainpipes we have laid in the forest (although we sometimes do that to make sure trails don't erode), but drainpipes manufactured by earthworms as they diligently tunnel, creating a system of slime-coated underground passageways.. They use these passageways to move quickly through the soil as they live their earthworm lives, but often they do not move quickly enough. Moles hunt these pencil-sized creatures down and snap them up as juicy snacks. If a mole catches more earthworms than it can eat, it immobilizes them with one bite and stores them in its den as living meals for later. That sounds unpleasant and it surely is unpleasant for the worms.

You usually see earthworms only after a steady downpour on a dreary fall day has turned the ground into a sea of mud. If you don't like that kind of rain, you're in good company, because the worms don't like it either. Water runs down into their underground accommodations and if they don't get up to the fresh air quickly enough, they drown miserably. But even reaching the surface doesn't guarantee their safety. If they crawl into a puddle, they end up suffering the fate they tried so hard to escape. And because water pools on hard-packed trails, in rainy weather you will find many of these watery graves.

This might be the time to make a small detour into forest survival techniques, as if you need food, catching earthworms makes a good alternative to hunting. And not only in bad weather. You can lure worms to the surface while the sun shines. To do this, you put a stick into the ground and drum on it. It vibrates like raindrops hitting the ground or, as another theory has it, like moles tracking down worms. Whichever it is, after a few minutes, the first worms will come crawling out of the ground. You can get the same effect by marching on the spot. Indeed, some enterprising birds and turtles have been seen to use the foot-stomping technique.

If you cook earthworms up with a little salt, they don't taste so bad—they're a bit reminiscent of chicken. There can be as many as two thousand earthworms to every ten square feet (one square meter) of soil. And so, if you are in a forest with earthworms around, there is no need to go hungry. This technique of attracting worms to the surface even has a name: worm grunting, apparently an age-old tradition in Florida. If you happen to visit Florida's Big Bend on the second Saturday in April, consider dropping into the Sopchoppy Worm Gruntin' Festival to see the technique in action and perhaps try it yourself. The worms charmed to the surface at Sopchoppy end up as fish bait.

Ants are also important members of the forest maintenance crew. Ants aerate soils, decompose wood, and disperse seeds. They also eat dead insects. Ants in Vermont forests build about an inch (2.5 centimeters) of new topsoil every 250 years and scatter the seeds of wildflowers such as trillium and bloodroot. Woodpeckers always look out for ants, as do bears, who like to get into their nests and eat the larvae and pupae, which they lick off their paws. Bears also like to lick foraging ants off the leaves of trees.

In the forests of the Pacific Northwest and California, millipedes are important decomposers. Millipedes look a bit like centipedes, except they have lots more legs. Two sets per body segment, to be exact, which makes them move in a sedate undulating wave that is fascinating to watch. Centipedes are carnivores, but millipedes are vegetarians, shredders that rip up leaves, extract the nutrients they need for themselves, and then deposit what remains for the next stage in the forest recycling process.

The yellow-spotted millipede of northern forests sports the universally understood mix of yellow and black that signals "Danger!" These millipedes contain cyanide and the only reason they don't kill themselves when they repel enemies is that they are immune to this poison. They also warn predators by giving off an almondy scent much like the cherry tree I mentioned earlier. Millipedes like dark, moist places and some of those who spend their time munching needles under the giant sequoias glow teal green: the brighter they glow, the more cyanide they contain. They do this just for the predators for these glow-in-the-dark millipedes are blind.

Further down the line of the decomposers come tiny creatures you will not see unless you get down on your hands and knees with a magnifying glass: springtails and mites. These two tiny critters work together. Springtails reduce organic matter to even finer particles, while mites mix the soil layers to bring these particles farther down into the soil, where fungi and bacteria can begin their work of releasing the nutrients they contain.

While you are down there checking for springtails, take a moment to dig down into the leaf litter. Can you see fine, whitish, slightly translucent threads criss-crossing the leaf litter and upper layers of the soil? You have found the fungal threads so important to forest health. Not only do tree roots interconnect with each other to transfer nutrients from strong trees to weaker ones, they also enter a mutually beneficial trading arrangement and communication service with fungi.

Fungi are very special organisms. Scientists don't really know how to classify them, so they have divided the world of living things into plants, animals, and fungi. Like animals, fungi cannot manufacture their own food, which makes them dependent on organic matter from other sources. Like insects, they have chitin in their cell walls, but they lack a central nervous system. Many of them are important tree allies. They help trees find food and water by growing around the trees' delicate root tips—sometimes even growing right into them. With their wide distribution and fluffy, cottony texture, the fungal threads greatly increase the roots' functional surface area so that significantly larger quantities of important nutrients reach the tree.

You could think of a fungal thread as a sort of inside-out digestive system. We break food down inside our guts. In fungi, this deconstruction of organic matter into the phosphorus, potassium, and nitrogen plants need to grow takes place on the outside of the fungal threads. If you look at the bags of fertilizer you can buy at your local store to feed the vegetables in your garden, you'll see numbers representing the nitrogen, phosphorus, and potassium they contain. The fungi provide a home-delivery service of these essential foods for trees. But, as the advertisements on television say, that is not all. The tips of fungal threads contain acid, which liquefies rock to release minerals such as copper and zinc that the trees need to stay healthy and grow strong. Tree-friendly fungi also prevent toxic substances like heavy metals from getting into their green partners and form an effective barrier against other fungi that might want to attack their trees.

Beyond food and protection, fungi provide trees with one more essential service that helps connect the forest ecosystem. Trees communicate through their root systems and warn each other about such things as insect attacks or imminent drought. As trees can't reach every corner of the forest with their roots, the interwoven fungal threads help relay the messages. Scientists talk of a forest internet or "wood wide web." Don't worry about breaking these threads as you dig. There are so many of them that if you break one, another thread will relay the messages and nutrients instead.

The fungi exact a high price for their services. A tree hands over up to one-third of its total food production to its hidden helpers, mostly in the form of sugar. One-third roughly equals the amount contained in the wood of the tree's trunk (the rest goes to growing branches, leaves, and fruit). Fungi use this concentrated form of energy not only for living day to day but also for growing their fruiting bodies.

The mushrooms you gather in the woods are like the apples on an apple tree. The fungus itself is composed of the delicate white threads growing through the ground, making connections with many plants. It can cover immense areas. The largest fungus found so far is a honey fungus in the Malheur National Forest in Oregon. Spread over three-and-a-half square miles (nearly one thousand hectares) and weighing somewhere between 7,500 and 35,000 tons, it is the largest known living organism on Earth, estimated to be many thousands of years old. This particular fungus is not very considerate when it comes to trees, however. It kills them so it can feed off them.

Mushrooms are the preferred food of the banana slug, a denizen of and important decomposer in the moist forests of the Pacific Northwest and along the California coast. Banana slugs grow up to ten inches (twenty-five centimeters) long, making them the second-largest slug in the world. The longest is a three-foot (ninety-centimeter sea slug), so, technically, banana slugs are the longest terrestrial slugs in the world. Banana slugs work their way methodically

Turkey tail, Sainte-Anne Falls, Quebec

through dead vegetable matter in forests where earthworms no longer ply their trade. They have a raspy tongue instead of teeth, which these yellow trash compactors use to scoop up everything from piles of scat to blackberries.

One of the most fascinating aspects of banana slugs is their slime. This liquid crystal (part liquid, part solid) is a multifunctional tool. The slime from banana slugs numbs the mouths of predators while also sticking their jaws together. Predators, reasonably enough, don't enjoy this and so tend to avoid eating the slugs. Crafty raccoons neutralize the slime effect by rolling their slugs in dirt before eating them. Native Americans popped banana slugs into their mouths to numb toothache. Jane won't do this because she thinks the mere idea of putting a slug into her mouth would probably be enough to stop her tooth from aching.

You shouldn't try this either, because slug slime can transmit disease and, also, that wouldn't be a very nice experience for the slug.

Banana slugs use their slime as a lubricant so they can glide over pokey twigs and sharp rocks on the forest floor, and as an adhesive so they can climb up the rough bark of trees. They use the scent in slime trails to find a mate. Slugs have both male and female organs so any banana slug will do. The slime also traps pine needles and other debris that gather at the back end of the slug as it slides through the forest. And so, the slug transports its own lunch box around, convenient for snacking at any time. And, as a bonus, slime is recyclable, so the banana slug can eat its own slime (or the slime of another banana slug) and reuse it.

Even if you don't see the banana slugs themselves on your hike (which you might not, as slugs like to keep cool and so will be hiding in dark places during the day), the sun glinting off their silvery trails betrays their presence. You might also see slime sparkling on the smooth trunks of trees such as beeches, where slugs like to graze on algae growing on the bark.

On your search for fungal threads and into the territory of slime trails, you might find some small clumps of low-growing plants that take advantage of the brisk trade going on between trees and their fungal partners: waxy silvery-white or pinkish stalks with a single hanging flower head that looks like a shaggy extension of the stem. These plants do not contain green chlorophyll to manufacture food, so they tap into the sugars the trees are delivering to their fungal associates.

The sugar stick is a particularly striking combination of ivory with vertical pink stripes. Apart from the sugar stick, this group includes the ghost plant, which is so white it almost glows, pinkish pinedrops, the yellowish to reddish Dutchman's pipe, also known as false beechdrops or pine sap, and a number of coralroot orchids. The presence of these plants indicate that the forest is in good health. Although they siphon off some of the sugar being traded, they do not damage the trees or the fungi, both of which seem happy to share.

And, of course, there are the fungi that are actively breaking dead and dying trees down, returning the nutrients contained in their wood to the ground to be taken up by the next generation of trees. You can spot some of the fungi that promote decay on standing trunks and on nurse logs. Their fruiting bodies are called conks. Delicate, frilly turkey tails have circles of varying colors radiating out over their surface. (If you see green ones, this is a sign algae are growing on them.) Sturdier shelf-like conks often come in shades of white, brown, and black. You may see beads of moisture on the surface of shelf fungi, particularly when they are having a growth spurt, which makes them look like they are sweating. The technical term is guttation, should you wish to impress your friends.

I can't leave this subject without mentioning slime molds. Slime molds used to be considered fungi but are now grouped in the catch-all kingdom of protists. Fascinating organisms, slime molds change shape and direction as they actively search out their food. On your travels you might encounter the bright yellow dog vomit slime mold, a particularly unappetizing-looking example that seeks out deciduous logs. Raspberry slime mold, to Jane at least, looks a bit like crimson caviar.

Like lichens, slime molds and fungi come in incredible forms and colors. And they have fascinatingly descriptive names: candlesnuff fungus, parrot whitecap, old man of the woods, dryad's saddle. Once you start looking for any of these, I promise you will find that your forest hikes are taking you much longer.

And all the while, the array of decomposers—large and small, animal, vegetable, and other—are reducing wood and leaves to particles tiny enough to be sifted underground, where temperatures are cooler, oxygen levels are lower, and the pace of decomposition slows. The first responders hand over the clean-up job to micro-organisms in the soil, including bacteria. These critters continue the work of eating and excreting begun by the above-ground decomposers. As the particles get ever-more minute, the next team takes over. Finally, the bodies of the decomposers themselves become part of the cycle.

Nutrients are released for the next generation of trees and carbon is buried deeper and deeper under the earth. For as long as the forest stays dark and cool, the carbon is heading for storage. If the forest is cleared and sunlight lands on the forest floor, the top-dwelling decomposers that work in a warm, oxygen-rich atmosphere reassert control and the carbon released in the decomposition process combines with oxygen to form the greenhouse gas carbon dioxide— just as it does when fossil forests are burned. Old, intact forests left to live their lives in peace do their part to ensure this does not happen.

~ 9 ~

Interpreting the Forest for Children

WHAT CAN YOU DO to make sure the children along on your hike are making as many fascinating discoveries as you are? I've never been a fan of dry-as-dust guided tours. Whether I'm in a city or a museum or out in nature, I get bored very quickly if the tour is all facts and no fun. And because school children often feel the same way, I came up with some different ideas for class outings in the forest. You might enjoy experimenting with some of these.

Why, for instance, should children learn to identify trees only by the shape and arrangement of their leaves and needles? Why not identify them by how they taste? And so, I let the children in the neighboring elementary school munch as well as look. For example, in the spring when the new growth is still tender and easy to chew, I get them to sample fresh spruce tips. They have a slightly citrusy taste with an undertone of resin. You can also brew the bright green growth into a tasty tea, another good way to make this tree memorable. Every year the local state forest agency organizes a youth competition in the woods and my students stand out thanks to their novel approach to tree identification. One class, when asked about the spruce trees in one of the group activities, put their tree-identification tools to the test by nibbling on them. The leader from the forest agency, who was supervising that station, laughed nervously and said, "That must be Mr. Wohlleben's group."

How about forest chewing gum all round to get started? I learned how to do this when I was a forestry trainee in 1984. On a tour through the southern part of Sweden, we visited commercial operations that demonstrated the benefits of using heavy machinery. Brochures were handed out at every stop, and on one occasion I was given a small flyer describing how to make chewing gum from spruce resin. I don't know what benefit the operation got from distributing this information, but the instructions worked and making forest chewing gum can be the highlight of the day.

First, of course, you need to find a spruce or pine tree that is dripping resin. Resin is like the tree's blood and when the bark is damaged, the tree bleeds just like you do when you get a cut in your skin. Of course, you shouldn't cut into your chosen tree just so you can make chewing gum. And that wouldn't work anyway, because you need a special kind of resin: a clear blob, already dried out and at least the size of your fingernail. If it meets all these criteria, you can put the piece of resin in your mouth and slowly warm it up. Test it carefully with your teeth every so often to see when it gets soft enough to chew. If you bite down on it too hard and too soon, the piece of resin will shatter, and then you will have to start all over again. If you attempt to do this with milky, cracked sap, it will turn to dust and leave a bitter taste in your mouth, literally.

Even if all goes as it should—that is, if the piece of resin gradually becomes soft enough that you can begin to shape it with your back teeth—it will taste bitter at first. Just spit these bitter-tasting substances out. (It would be thoughtful to spit into a tissue you could dispose of safely at home.) That might sound gross, but you are out in the forest and, apart from the other members of your group and a few birds, no one is looking. As the resin loses its bitter edge, it gradually transforms into a piece of soft, rosy-pink forest chewing gum that doesn't stick to your teeth. It's a nice little surprise if you're looking for a child-friendly activity. You do need clear, hard resin, however. If you settle for resin that is still soft, the fun will turn to frustration. Soft resin stays sticky when you chew it. It adheres to your teeth and you will probably get to enjoy it for longer than you intended as you try to get it out from between them. When you don't want to chew the gum any longer, you can get rid of it by returning it to nature. Perhaps you can simply stick the resin back onto the tree you got it from.

I'm not making a case for identifying everything by tasting it, because there are also poisonous species in the world of trees. However, once you've positively identified a spruce, oak, or willow with the help of a field guide, experiencing the tree with all your senses will help fix your learning into place. And this is especially true for children. They'll find it easier to remember the tart taste and thirst-quenching qualities of a spruce's fresh new growth than the tree's dry Latin name.

It's the same with beeches. The fresh leaves in May are also tender and slightly tart, but without the resinous undertone of spruce. They make a great addition to a forest salad, but you must make it and eat it on the spot. Don't add the dressing until just before you're ready to eat, because the little leaves wilt almost immediately. If you harvest leaves from the lower branches of a large tree, you will not do it any harm. Indeed, you will find yourself in excellent company: many species of beetles, to say nothing of deer, are doing the same thing as they enjoy these tasty treats.

You can eat the new growth from many native trees. Whether they are maple, birch, oak, linden, pine, or larch, all the new green growth tastes good and each has its own distinctive flavor. You could just nibble your way through nature's yummy field guide. But when I say, "many trees," there are exceptions. Needles from yews, for example, are easy to confuse with needles from firs, but unlike fir needles, they are highly toxic. Therefore, you should positively identify any tree before helping yourself to a snack from its branches.

If you're not comfortable having the children nibbling directly on the trees, don't worry. The forest air can also have a distinctive taste. Get the children to open their mouths and stick out their tongues. Then ask them if they're aware of any flavors. Jane tried this on a recent forest walk and got a bitter taste in her mouth, but the woman standing next to her got a taste of clear, cool water. I wonder what flavors your group will get.

You can also experiment with sound. Get the children to close their eyes and tell you the farthest-away sound they can hear. Then the closest. Do the sounds come from animals, plants, or features in the landscape, such as flowing water? Do they come from inside the forest or beyond the trees?

We shouldn't overlook our sense of smell. There are lots of opportunities to intensify forest scents for the children. If you rub Douglas fir needles between your fingers, they release a fragrance reminiscent of candied orange peel. The flowers of bigleaf maples smell of vanilla, and the tannin produced by oaks smells slightly bitter. Poplar fluff has a balmy smell that reminds Jane of camping expeditions in Saskatchewan. The bark on young yellow birch smells distinctly minty. The twigs of cherries smell of bitter almond when you snap them in two. Encourage children to inhale deeply in different kinds of forests. Which ones do they like the smell of best? Pines and oaks, or aspens and beeches? Maybe they are picking up on some of the messages the trees are sharing amongst themselves.

As you're snapping twigs open to see how they smell, you can get the children to look inside. Is the center dark or cream colored, or is the twig solid all the way through? If the center has a distinct color, what shape is it: round, star-shaped (Jane's favorite), or something else? All these shapes and colors inside the twig can help you identify the trees you're looking at if you have a good identification key to follow, which you can find in books or online. The keys will ask you for other clues, as well, such as how the leaves attach to the stem and what the bark on the twig looks like. If you don't want to go as far as tree identification, just enjoy the patterns and make a game out of it by having the children guess which patterns the twigs will reveal when you snap them open.

Some parts of the forest invite you to touch them. You can get children to stroke the bright green tips of spruce branches. They are almost irresistible because they feel so silky soft. You can make a game out of "shaking hands with" a mature Douglas fir. This is a good winter activity because it's best done with gloves. The craggy bark of Douglas fir has tiny hairs that can poke through skin and make you itchy.

The surface of grand fir, hemlock, and cedar bark is less craggy and smoother to the touch.

Children don't have to get the feel of the forest from actively touching the trees. You can also let the air in the forest wash over you. Right at the beginning of this book, I mentioned that stepping into the cool green of the forest feels like entering an underwater world. If you've ever swum in a stream, a lake, or out in the ocean, you've probably noticed places where the water feels cooler and warmer depending on the currents running through it. You can feel something similar as the breeze blows through the forest: patches where you feel sun-warmed and patches that are refreshingly cool.

Invite children to walk along with their arms spread wide to feel how the temperature changes. This works even better if they shut their eyes but that can lead to running into trees, so they'd best keep their eyes open to see where they are going. They can pretend they're drifting along through an ocean of trees like a forest of kelp breaking the breeze into a series of different currents, some hot from the sun above and others cool from the depths of the forest. They can choose the spot where they feel most comfortable and stop there for a break before deciding what they want to do next.

As you get to know the forest better, you could consider taking a small section and creating a forest diary to track the time of year when the conifers start growing new green tips in spring or when the deciduous trees start losing their leaves in fall. When do the trilliums appear and when does the skunk cabbage bloom? When do you see the first dragonflies? Or hear the tree frogs peeping? Climate change is affecting the timing of these seasonal events. You can help local citizen science groups by noting the changes you are experiencing. And you can take memories of the forest home with you by making a collection of photographs, creating a scrapbook, and pressing leaves and flowers.

One of the best things about an excursion into the woods is taking a break and, especially with children, you shouldn't skip these. I've done lots of tours with elementary or primary school children, and I've noticed it works best to stick with the timetable used during the children's normal school day. I've discovered that if I get carried away and spend too long on the experiments and games, the little ones, especially, quickly lose interest and begin to get grouchy. As soon as they've had a quick break and a snack, you can win them back with a new activity—or simply set them free to play.

~ 10 ~

Forest Activities with Children

FOR CHILDREN, EXPERIENCING the forest isn't only about learning. The forest can also be a big messy playground with tree branches instead of swing sets, puddles instead of wading pools, and carpets of moss instead of park benches. Often children appreciate the forest most when you let them do their own thing, especially when you let them get dirty.

We grown-ups usually think of dirt as gross and disgusting, and under normal circumstances that's as it should be. Household dirt—oil, paint, rust, dust, or, of course, pet feces—can pose health risks and should quickly be removed from clothes and hands. Soil and crumbly humus, however, are not a danger to your health. Even the green algae coating a tree trunk, which gets slimy when it rains and ends up on your jacket if you lean up against it, is nothing to worry about. It's the same stuff as seaweed in the ocean.

Despite the attraction of green spaces, there's something inside us that fights against too-close contact with nature, as I discovered when I went for a walk in the forest with a group of teenagers from an alternative high school. Wearing white sneakers and carrying cell phones, they didn't even want to go into the forest at first. When they did go in, most of them picked up a fallen branch to use as a walking stick so they wouldn't slip while making their way between the trees. But they didn't pick the branches up with their bare hands. To my astonishment, they took out paper tissues and used them to keep their hands clean as they reached for their improvised hiking poles. After a couple of days in Hümmel, I no longer recognized them. I had incorporated a few survival activities into the daily routine and now they were challenging each other to snack on beetle larvae.

So, it's important that children go out into the forest wearing clothes they can get dirty—and that they have permission to do just that. Then the fun can begin. Who's up for giving the trees faces? All you have to do is apply some nice soft mud onto a section of bark. Then, using a twig as a paintbrush, you can "paint" eyes, nose, and mouth onto the tree trunks. Soon half the forest will be filled with fun faces that will last for at least a few days and perhaps even until the next forest outing.

Or how about experimenting with a forest telephone? It only works over short distances, but that's what makes it useful, at least for birds that make their nests in cavities high up in the trees. For most birds, squirrels and martens pose the deadliest threats to their babies. These animals climb trees and try to pluck the helpless youngsters out of nest cavities using the sharp claws on their front paws. If you're a bird parent, what can you do? Not much. You can try mounting a courageous attack by flying out at the aggressor. There's a small chance you might annoy the intruder enough for it to leave you in peace. Sometimes, however, predators target birds while they sleep.

Birds can fly away when danger threatens, but only if they have enough advance warning. Luckily, they can depend on a wake-up call via the forest telephone, which, in this case, consists of the tree's trunk. Wood transmits sound incredibly well, which is why it is used to make musical instruments. On the giant instrument that is an old trunk, the claws of squirrels and martens play a melody that signals impending death. As they climb, their scratching noises are easy to hear inside the trunk's cavities. Despite the built-in early-warning system, the birds have only a few seconds to react to the approaching danger.

Children can test how the telephone (or, it might be more accurate to say, the alarm system) works using a tree trunk lying on the ground. To do this, a child kneels at one end and presses an ear to the bark, while at the other end a child sends a message by tapping a rock against the trunk. The child at the receiving end counts how many taps they hear. It's even more realistic if instead of tapping, the child makes scratching noises with the rock. Then the child at the end of the telephone will hear the same kind of warning signal the birds hear.

Or perhaps the children would prefer a bit of forest music. I don't mean birdsong or the rustling of branches in the treetops, but real music they make themselves. Are you worried that might disturb the sense of being out in nature? Read on and you'll see that what I propose is grounded in nature itself. Quite apart from that, sound in the forest is not necessarily disruptive. In fact, at times, it can be quite useful.

Does this situation sound familiar? You're walking through the forest with children and after a while the volume goes up. Perhaps the youngsters have started play-ing tag or are shouting to announce they've discovered a small critter, or perhaps they're simply squealing with plea-sure. As an adult, your immediate response is "Shush. Not so loud!" But why? Does it really disturb the deer and the chipmunks when people are being loud? Wild animals do like quiet, but not because they are overly sensitive to noise. It's because when a storm rages through the treetops or a deluge descends, they can't hear anything above the wind and the rain, not even coyotes or cougars on the prowl. And that can put them in mortal danger. That's why forest crit-ters love calm, dry weather when they can hear every twig-snapping approach from far away.

Therefore, the loud noises people make don't set for-est animals on edge, because instead of filling the forest with surround sound, they come from just one direction. They also signal to large mammals such as deer that their greatest enemies are not out on the prowl. That would be us, specifically those of us who hunt. Even in places where predators such as wolves and wildcats are slowly returning, their camouflaged human equivalents are a thousand times more numerous. And so, it's hardly surprising that wild ani-mals in our forests focus their fear on two-legged hunters.

In areas where predatory mammals such as bears, cou-gars, or wolves are about, it's also better to make noise than to keep quiet. Large though they are, these animals also prefer to give people a wide berth. Researchers in the Santa Cruz Mountains in California recently found that even someone quietly reading poetry is enough to make moun-tain lions avoid the area. But just in case the bears are not attuned to poetry or are hard of hearing, most informa-tional brochures suggest animated conversations or bear bells to advertise your approach. When we walk along trails singing happily or chatting loudly, we let our fellow creatures know we're not out stalking them and we're giving them the opportunity to slip away if they would prefer to avoid us.

But back to making music, rather than just noise, in the forest. Let's start with the very easiest instrument you can learn to play: a beech leaf. If you hold your thumbs together lengthwise, you'll see there's a little gap between them. Place the leaf firmly between the first and second joints (counted down from the nail) to make it taut. You are ready to play your very first forest instrument. Here's how you do it. Press your lips against the gap between your thumbs and blow hard. You will hear a hoarse cheeping sound that can be quite loud. You can make the note higher or lower and smoother or raspier by adjusting how hard you blow, but that's about it for the leaf's musical range.

How about something more challenging? I remember willow whistles well from my childhood when my family used to go on multiday hiking trips with another family. I was fascinated by how you can conjure up such a beautiful toy using simple materials found in nature. Here's how it's done. You need a pocketknife and a fresh green branch from a willow. Choose a branch about as thick as your finger. It should be four to six inches (ten to fifteen centimeters) long and have no side branches or other imperfections along its length. Halfway down, carefully make a single cut through the bark down to the wood all the way around.

At the end you're going to put in your mouth, make an incision on one side to create a hole like the one that allows air into a recorder. To do this, cut across the bark at a ninety-degree angle about a half-inch (one centimeter) from the end until you get down to the wood. Make a short, angled cut along the branch to meet the first cut. This second cut should also go down to the wood. Then free the half of the branch you have been working on from the wood beneath, removing the bark so it comes off in one piece. To make this easier, tap the bark with the handle of your knife (but not too hard; you don't want to break it). The father of the family we hiked with used to chant a German phrase like a mantra as he did this. The closest English equivalent would probably be "Eenie, meenie, miney, mo, the willow whistle is ready to go." (Just in case you want to follow a tried-and-true family tradition!) You now have a hollow tube of bark with a hole in it.

The bark loosens most easily in early spring when a particularly large quantity of water is moving up the tree. You can help the process along by moistening the small section of wood in your mouth every so often and then tapping on it again. Once you have removed the bark, saw a half-inch (one centimeter) nub off the exposed wood and then use the blade of your knife to flatten it in one side. Now push it down into the upper section of the bark tube with the air hole in it with the flat side of the wood facing the hole. All done.

If you insert the section of branch with the exposed wood into the whistle from below and blow into the instrument, you can raise and lower the pitch by sliding the section of wood up and down. The result will amaze you, and with a bit of practice you can play whole songs. Children find the whole process fascinating. It makes a great activity if you're out in the woods and the children are getting a bit out of hand.

If you want children to slow down and focus, you can also try this scavenging activity. Mark off an area with small branches and invite them to find interesting objects to put

Green anole, Lake Livingston State Park, Texas

inside. A piece of lichen or moss, perhaps, or a small section of bark where a sapsucker has drilled openings. A twig etched with trails left by beetle larvae or a berry, a pinecone, or some seeds. Children soon learn to leave anything too delicate to move (spider webs strung between branches, the fluffy seed clocks of wildflowers) and to respect the right of small critters to roam freely in their forest home (lady beetles, lizards, and ants). Invite them to consider what each find reveals about the bustle of life around them, and how each contributes to the living systems of the forest by providing food, shelter, or protection. They can take a moment to thank the forest for all the beautiful things it has provided and tell the forest they will be good stewards in the future. Encourage the children to leave the objects so the forest can recycle them.

~ 11 ~

The Forest at Night

YOU CAN SHARE the experience of the forest at night with children. First of all, though, think of your own comfort level. One way to approach this is to ask yourself where you feel more at ease: in a busy pedestrian area in a big city during the day or alone in a dark forest at night? And because you can probably guess where I'm headed with this question, I invite you to test this for yourself. Our senses and instincts scream "Danger!" whenever there's nothing for them to process except for a few eerie noises, none of which we recognize. Is something lurking over there in the shadows? Is that cracking in the undergrowth a large animal coming closer? If this is where you are, it might be best to experiment with a nighttime forest walk on your own or in the company of friends before bringing children along with you.

Even I feel a slight sense of unease occasionally, though I know perfectly well nothing is going to happen to me. It's the genetic legacy passed down by our ancestors messing with our minds. Although there were times when outlaws roamed the woods, or even further back in history, times when saber-toothed tigers searched for easy prey, today, statistically speaking, the forest is the safest place to be at any time of day or night. What kind of a thief would want to lurk behind a tree waiting to pounce on a hiker wandering by? Depending on which trails the would-be robber was staking out, they'd run the risk of getting covered in mildew before a worthwhile victim showed up. A pedestrian zone teeming with potential targets offers a much better bet. And most forest animals prefer to avoid people if they can.

And so, spending time in the forest at night makes for a particularly safe and beautiful experience. As darkness descends, the noises of civilization recede. The sound of rush-hour traffic fades away, lawn mowers fall silent, and construction sites go quiet. The only greeting from civilization is the occasional airplane flying into the night. Why is this absence of sound important in the forest? It's important because only in real quiet do you realize how far sound travels, and to have an authentic experience in nature, you need to immerse yourself in natural sounds. I am regularly reminded how difficult this is when I go out into the forest with camera crews. The crews like to record background noises for atmosphere: a couple of minutes of treetops rustling and birds singing to play during video segments without dialogue. These sound sequences are important because out in the field acoustic disturbances usually occur every few minutes, mostly from cars, trucks, or airplanes.

If you want an undisturbed experience in the forest at night, you have two options. The first takes you to a valley in the mountains. Because mountains do a good job of blocking sound, uninhabited valleys are very quiet, although you will still hear the occasional airplane passing over in the night sky. The second (much easier) option is to take a walk when the wind is blowing gently through the trees. When a light breeze whispers through the leaves, when branches rustle as they rub against one another and tree trunks creak gently as they bend, the sounds of the trees not only mask other sources of sound, they also create the most perfect symphony a nighttime forest can offer. Under these conditions, you hear what thousands of generations before us heard: sounds that provided the background music to countless campfires around which Stone Age peoples gathered. On walks like these I always experience a special sense of freedom and timelessness.

To fully enjoy your nighttime rambles, I suggest sticking to the trails, or you could end up with a sharp stick poking you in the eye—literally. In coniferous forests in particular, lots of broken-off branches, about as thick as your finger and down low on the trunks, pose a serious risk of injury. Despite that danger, I urge you to resist the temptation to take out your flashlight. The contraption will catapult you back into civilization immediately and heighten your fear of the unknown by making everything outside the circle of light much more difficult to see. It will also set your night vision back by hours. Your eyes adapt well to seeing in the dark, but they take a long time to do so. During the day, small cones on your retina process light. They are not particularly sensitive to light, because there is plenty of it outside and in brightly lit rooms. At night, in contrast, rods come into their own. They are the cones' poor cousins and can process only black-and-white images, which explains the saying, "All cats are gray in the dark." Because our eyes cannot process color in the dark, and because it is even darker in the forest than in open spaces, it makes sense to give your eyes a chance to adapt.

If you do end up needing artificial light, it's best to use red light. Red light has little effect on our eyes' ability to adapt to the dark, which is why, for example, astronomers use red light when observing the night sky through their telescopes. (Incidentally, you can buy red lights quite cheaply at outdoor equipment outlets.) Use your red light just like a regular flashlight—and remember, as with a regular flashlight, it's not polite to shine it right into the eyes of any animals you might find. You can also see more at night by choosing the best times to go out: a cloudless night with a full moon is an ideal time to start collecting night-hiking experiences. On nights such as these, the moon shines so brightly you could read a newspaper by its light.

What's up in the forest at night, anyway? Is that when everything really comes to life? Not quite. At least not when it comes to the trees. They are slumbering in a deep, restorative sleep and, just like us when we go to bed, taking a break from daily tasks. They're not producing sugar through photosynthesis so the action inside the trunks and crowns slows down. This affects oxygen levels in the air, because the trees are still burning sugar and other carbohydrates and taking in oxygen to do so. As I mentioned earlier, trees are not simply suppliers of oxygen, though people quickly reduce them to this (after timber production, of course). No, indeed. Trees breathe through hundreds of thousands of microscopic openings on the undersides of their leaves and needles and in their bark. During the day, trees produce oxygen as a byproduct when they use sunlight to help break down water and carbon dioxide and process them into sugar. But at night, just as we do, the giants draw on the stores of energy under their skin (which is to say their bark) and exhale large amounts of carbon dioxide. And so healthy forest air is just a little bit less healthy at night, but the difference is so slight that you need not worry about it.

I find a recent scientific discovery especially touching: trees fall asleep when it's dark. A research team from Austria and Finland scanned the crowns of birches with a laser and were surprised to discover that as soon as it became dark, the trees relaxed their leaves and branches, and as night progressed, they hung down still farther. The difference between their position at night and in the light of day could be as much as four inches (ten centimeters). It's not yet known if the trees are woken up in the morning by the rising sun or by an internal clock. Scientists have also recently discovered that it takes a while for plants to adjust to light and restart photosynthesis in the morning, just as you might blink a few times before you open your eyes wide and get out of bed.

Another process you won't notice is that trees get fatter at night. Just a little bit, but enough that scientists can measure the difference. This happens when the leaves no longer accept water flowing into the trunk from the roots. After all, the roots are now fast asleep. As soon as sugar production starts again with the first rays of the morning sun, the tree's paunch disappears.

As it gets darker, nighttime specialists such as bats and moths take over from the day shift of songbirds and butterflies, and many mammals that take it easy during the day rouse themselves to hunt and forage. They have developed effective night-hunting strategies. Take those bats and moths I just mentioned. Bats locate moths at night using ultrasound. If you look at a moth closely, you will see it's furry. Its hunters are the reason for its fuzzy coat. The rough surface of a moth's body and wings breaks up the bat's ultrasound signal so the flying mammals can't find them. One of the largest moths in North America, the beautiful green luna moth goes even further with this shape shifting. It has trailing ribbons at the ends of its wings that are thought to confuse bats by making it difficult for them to know which part of the moth to target when they attack. In addition to these clever camouflages, moths have developed excellent hearing for sounds in the upper register, which means they can hear when bats are hunting them and know when to take evasive action.

Fireflies are another delight of the night forest. Jane was thrilled to have one fly right in front of her one night in Texas. It came so close she could see its abdomen all lit up. A firefly's light is the product of a chemical reaction. Nearly 100 percent of the energy produced is given off as light. This compares with a standard lightbulb, where 90 percent of the energy produced when it lights up is given off as heat. Fireflies glow so brightly because their flash is first intensified as it passes over a layer of reflective cells inside the insect and then scattered by an array of transparent, jagged scales on the exterior of its abdomen. After studying the design of fireflies' exterior scales, scientists created an overlay for standard LED lights that increased the efficiency of the lights by more than 50 percent.

There are over 150 species of fireflies in North America. One, known as the Chinese lantern, floats on the breeze. Most fly, lighting up the forest like sparks from a campfire in shades of blue, yellow, and green. Each species leaves its own signature in the sky. The big dipper firefly, the most common in North America, produces a J-shaped flash pattern. Other flash patterns look like the dots and dashes of Morse code. Some fireflies even synchronize their lights in a complicated shared code as males in flight communicate with females, who flash back from the ground. Fireflies love areas around water and a kayak offers a good way to view them in the areas they frequent. After all, you don't want to be treading on the creatures you have come to view.

Fireflies are not the only living organisms glowing at night. If you're lucky, you might come across some of the glow-in-the-dark mushrooms that break down lignin in wood: bleeding fairy helmets, jack-o'-lanterns, or bitter oyster mushrooms. No one knows why they glow. They might do it to attract nighttime browsers. If an animal eats them, that animal may then spread their spores to another part of the forest. Jack-o'-lanterns glow using the same chemical reaction that fireflies use to produce their light. When this light is emitted by mushrooms, it is sometimes referred to as "foxfire."

Then there are the animals and plants that do not light up like fireflies, but fluoresce. That is, they absorb short-wave ultraviolet light and emit it back at a wavelength we can see. Recent research has revealed that flying squirrels turn bubblegum pink under ultraviolet light. What benefit does this give them? We don't really know. Maybe these tiny squirrels are trying to blend in with lichens on trees that also process light this way. Or maybe they are mimicking predatory owls, which fluoresce in a variety of colors. The wings of the northern saw-whet owl, for example, fluoresce a bright raspberry pink. The newer the owl's feathers, the more intense the color.

Incidentally, you can find flying squirrels in many forests in North America, where they are most active at night. Strictly speaking, they do not fly but glide thanks to membranes along each side of their body. When they stretch out their legs, they assume the same shape as those people who jump out of planes in wingsuits. When flying squirrels glide, they use their legs to steer and their tails as a brake, an accessory not available to their human counterparts.

If you'd like to discover other strange colors emitted by creatures when they fluoresce, go out armed with a black light to see what you can find. You likely won't be lucky enough to spot a flying squirrel but, if you are in the South, you might find a scorpion glowing bluish-green on the forest floor. We are creatures of the day and we know little about what the night forest looks like to all the nocturnal animals that move around in it. One thing we do know, however, is that it is a much more magical place than the one we see with human eyes.

There are also gruesome horror stories happening at night—gruesome for the actors involved, that is, not for us. California turret spiders, relatives of tarantulas, hunt at night. Instead of making sticky webs to capture their prey, they build turrets, where they lie in wait. They line the insides of their castle-like towers with silk and coat the outsides with mud, moss, and leaves. The spiders spend their days in burrows up to six inches (fifteen centimeters) underground. At dusk, they climb up to their watchtowers, waiting to sense the vibrations from a passing pill bug or beetle. Then the spider jumps out and impales its prey with its fangs. These relatively long-lived spiders are homebodies and can live for sixteen years, all in the same turret.

On the subject of spiders, here's something you can try—if you dare! Take your regular flashlight and slowly scan the area. You may well shine your light on what look like bright blue or purple diamonds sparkling on the forest floor. These are the eyes of wolf spiders. Don't worry, they're not dangerous and have no interest in you unless you bother them. Wolf spider mothers protect their babies by carrying them

Barred owl, Highlands Hammock State Park, Florida

around on their backs. If one falls off, she will stop and wait for it to climb back up. They are the only spiders known to care for their young this way.

No catalog of night animals would be complete without mentioning those silent nighttime hunters, the owls. I never cease to be fascinated by the flight of owls. Their feathers are slightly fringed at the edges, which allows them to fly in absolute silence as they search for scuttling mice or sleeping birds. Owls appear and disappear like nocturnal ghosts. Their prey has no clue they're coming, only realizing their end is near when it's too late. Jane once watched at a local county fair as a long line of children lay down on the ground with their eyes closed and an owl flew over them. The children heard nothing, but they knew the owl was passing because they felt the air move.

Giveaways for owls in the forest can be "white-wash" on their favorite perching trees and pellets full of hard-to-digest bones, feathers, and teeth lying on the ground beneath. If you dissect an owl pellet, you can see what the owl has been eating. You might even be able to reconstruct a complete rodent skeleton from the fragments. As owl pellets can contain diseases, it's best to order sterilized pellets online if you want to pursue this line of inquiry.

The owls you might find on a forest hike range from the enormous great horned owl to the minute northern saw-whet owl, with a wide selection in between. You're more likely to hear them than see them, but occasionally you might spot a pair of eyes looking at you from a hollow in a tree or from high up on a branch. If you hear a hoot that sounds like "Who cooks for you? Who cooks for you-all?" you are hearing a barred owl. You can try hooting back to see if you can engage it in conversation. Barred owls are among the most vocal of owls, sometimes making sounds a bit like a troop of monkeys exchanging pleasantries. You can mostly hear barred owls at night, but not all owls are nocturnal. The darker an owl's eyes, the more likely it is a nighttime hunter.

If you don't feel quite up to a night hike, you can always look at the webcam footage available in some park and campground visitor centers. You will be amazed at the animals that become active while we are fast asleep.

~ 12 ~

Seasonal Walks

IT IS NOT JUST nighttime that changes the face of the forest. The same forest can look distinctly different depending on the time of year, so you can vary your forest experience by walking the same trails in different seasons. A journey through time rather than space. And if your interest in a forest diary was piqued by my earlier mention of forest activities with children, these walks would be a wonderful time to add to your collection of forest impressions to track changes from year to year.

WINTER HAS MANY advantages. The forest is particularly quiet. The hikers are few and far between, and, even more importantly, the mosquitoes and midges (tiny biting flies), though still there, are peacefully slumbering as they wait for spring to arrive.

Personally, I feel doubly happy when the snow falls. First, I like to pull on my winter boots and stomp through the white snow in all its pristine glory. Second, I can unravel many mysteries when snow blankets the ground, at least those mysteries that have to do with animals. For at this time of year, their tracks are clearly visible. Not all snow-falls are equal when it comes to tracks. The first snowfall of the season is particularly revealing. The animals, not yet in winter mode, are more active than after a prolonged period of cold. Start your tour of discovery in the morning, because by midday the sun may have melted the tracks, or a brisk wind may have come by and filled them with snow. Take your camera or phone along to take pictures of what you find, so you can identify the tracks using a guidebook or website when you are back in the comfort of home.

Usually the only white you find is snow. Under specific weather conditions, however, shadowy beings enter the picture, conjuring up tufts of icy white hair on branches rotting on the forest floor. This hair-like ice is the frozen breath of fungi. It works like this: fungi break down the wood, digest it, and, just like we do, exhale water vapor, carbon dioxide, and other organic compounds. These exhalations freeze as soon as they meet with the cold outside air. As the fungi's next breath pushes from behind, gauzy skeins of hair-like ice form. If you touch these ice hairs, they melt instantly into a couple of droplets of water. Fungi can't operate in frozen wood, because when the wood freezes, they freeze, too. That's why you find hair ice only when the temperature outside hovers just below freezing and the temperature inside the wood remains slightly above freezing.

ISN'T FEBRUARY AN awful month, at least when it comes to going outside? The trees are bare, the weather's often bad, and thanks to climate change there may be barely any snow. Instead, day after day of rain makes the ground so wet that mud splashes up your pant legs with every step you take. The long wait for spring has reached its peak and

Hair ice, Rasar State Park, Washington

the collective mood has reached its correspondingly low-
est point. But this somewhat depressing and distorted view
of things, brought on by the winter blues, doesn't reflect
what's going on in the forest. If you take a moment to pull
yourself together and set out on a walk, you will soon find
out that this supposedly bleak time of year is not boring
and drained of color. Quite the contrary.

Take mosses, for example. They grow on the lower parts of
tree trunks and cover exposed roots making it look as though
green octopuses have taken over the forest floor and trees
are now sprouting up amongst them. At this time of year, the
contrast between brown leaves, gray-brown bark, and the
glowing green of this mossy carpet is particularly intense.

The birds that have stuck around for the winter are
becoming more active as they search for mates and defend

their territories. And so, especially toward the end of the month, you often hear woodpeckers drumming loudly. That is their way of singing and letting competitors know this part of the forest is already taken. Hares also get into the spirit of spring, sometimes as early as January. Female hares are picky and look for the best boxers as mates. When the males are fighting for the female's attention, the fur really flies, and if you look closely, you can see tufts lying around their battleground.

February is also the month some bushes start to wake up. Take hazel, for example. The male catkins hang down from the branches like tiny tails and release pollen, which can cause the first seasonal attacks of hay fever for people with an allergy to it. You can barely see the red female flowers because they are hardly larger than the head of a pin. Hazel twigs are so flexible at this time of year that you can easily tie them in knots. I'm not sure why you would want to do this, but now you know and you can add this to your list of fun forest facts.

While deciduous trees slumber on, conifers native to northern climes stand poised to get going. In their homeland, they have to make the most of each warm day in the short growing season, so they are ready at the starting line much sooner than their leafy colleagues. You can't tell by looking at them, because the buds with the new growth are still closed, but if you come across an area where trees have recently been cut down, take a moment to look at the stumps. In warm weather, you'll see drops of resin being pushed out where the bark meets the wood. The presence of fresh water in the tree indicates a new growing season is beginning. The pressure pushing the water upward will increase through March and April, and not even a cold snap will slow it down. That's why maple sap is harvested at this time of year. As soon as leaves unfold and fresh growth sprouts, the pressure decreases and the wood dries out a bit.

What trees really like at this time of year is a thick covering of snow that melts slowly so moisture seeps into the ground, where it can be stored for a long time. Then, if the weather turns dry, the trees can draw on this water long into the summer.

BY EARLY SPRING, the deciduous forests are greening up once again. Thanks to climate change, trees lower down in the valleys have shifted the time of leaf break forward to April. For deciduous trees, growing leaves is an enormous feat of strength that almost completely exhausts the reserves stockpiled the previous summer. And so, they wait patiently to be sure that spring really has arrived, and they unfurl their new leaves only when all danger of frost has passed. But trees can make mistakes too, and in upper elevations, in particular, it can freeze into June. When that happens, the fresh green growth turns brown and hangs limply from the branches, and for beeches and the like, a tough fight for survival begins. Everything must start over and not every tree has sufficient reserves to leaf out a second time.

This is a tricky time of year for trees. As they transition from a restful winter to being more active in spring, they are pushing more water than usual up their trunks. Early in the season, the pressure is so high that if you were to place a stethoscope against the bark, you would hear the water shooting up inside. No one knows exactly how these green giants pump themselves full of water. Transpiration, osmosis, capillary action—none of these alone or in combination completely explain the process. Because of all the moisture, the bark no longer adheres so closely to the wood, and therefore the trees are particularly susceptible to damage. And because of all the available moisture, fungi and bacteria quickly infect any wounds, which makes it very difficult for the trees to heal.

AT MOST TIMES of the year, deciduous woodlands are too dark for flowers to bloom on the forest floor, but in May, the forest floor can be strewn with flowers. Where I live in Germany, for instance, the thick crowns of beeches and oaks allow only 3 percent of the sun's light to penetrate to the forest floor. That's not enough for most plants to survive. However, a small window in spring gives tiny plants a chance. When it warms up toward the end of March, the delicate growth of wood anemones, buttercups, and wild garlic pushes its way up through the previous fall's dead leaves.

These "spring ephemerals," as they are called, must get a move on. They need to grow, bloom, form seeds, and put away reserves for next spring, all before it gets too dark here below. The big trees are still sleeping but will slowly begin to wake when April is almost over. It will take until the middle of May before the green canopy finally closes in. And so, the colorful plants have barely two months to get all those things done that most plants can take all summer to achieve. If you look at it that way, wood anemones and the like are the sprinters of the forest.

In North American forests, spring jewels include red and white trilliums, orange trout lilies, and lady's slipper orchids. Purple and white violets hug the ground and red columbines grow tall to welcome hummingbirds. In damp, shady areas, slightly prehistoric-looking jacks-in-the-pulpit unfurl their green sheaths to reveal dramatic purple and white stripes.

Maples in eastern forests cast a reddish-orangey hue

across the forest. For maximum reproductive success, they need to get their wind-pollinated male and female flowers out there in the breeze before leaves close the canopy. Understory trees and shrubs also put on a show, this time for the pollinators, before they are cast into shade: white dogwoods twinkling like constellations, cucumber magnolias calling out for sap beetles to visit, the peachy tones of flame azaleas, and, a little later, the deep pink of redbuds.

Also in May, certain large insects emerge from the ground, such as rare stag beetles, which live secretively and hidden in rotten wood. The larvae spend three to eight years contentedly munching through crumbling wood before pupating and emerging into the light of day as impressive-looking little stags. The adult beetles live for only a few weeks, just long enough to mate and lay eggs. The males use their antlers, which are not actually antlers but over-sized jaws, to fight rivals. These proud knights aren't dangerous, and they don't have enough strength in their jaws to bite. To feed, they lick tree sap that flows after the females (which can bite!) make a few small wounds in a tree's bark. After mating, the females lay a few eggs around the roots of dying or dead trees, and then the beetle parents depart for beetle heaven. Because stag beetles depend on dead wood, they are considered critically endangered. In modern commercial forests, there's little space for rotting oaks and other deciduous trees. There is, however, an alternate refuge for this beetle: wooden fence posts or the stumps of dead fruit trees. If you have those in your yard, you can leave them there for these little guys.

These beetles are a good example of how subjectively we see the world. If the larval stage accounts for up to 99 percent of the stag beetle's life, wouldn't it make more sense to name it after this stage of its development? The problem is we don't see it during its larval phase. We see it only in its short-lived mating form. That makes it more difficult for us to understand it and leads us to feel sorry for it for the wrong reasons. The mayfly is another example. It flies only in order to mate. Before this brief act, however, it lives in streams and ponds for a year. We pity it for its short life, even though it lives a relatively long time for an insect. Mayflies may live short lives in their mating form, but what they lack in winged longevity they more than make up for in numbers. Mayflies can swarm so densely that they show up on weather radars and completely cover the windshields and hoods of stationary cars.

A population explosion of insects sounds pretty horrifying. I once experienced just that in a stand of oaks in the woodland I manage. The trees were infested with small green moths called oak leaf rollers. Millions of caterpillars were nibbling on and digesting the freshly unfurled leaves. If you eat a lot, there's something else you must do a lot of. With a single oak leaf roller caterpillar, all you get is a few tiny little round black specks, but when a whole army of them is munching away, you get an uninterrupted deluge of tens of thousands of these tiny pellets. The noise these pellets make when they fall sounds like torrential rain—and it goes on uninterrupted for weeks. Needless to say, walking through a forest infested in this way is not particularly pleasant. In North America, similar infestations of gypsy moth and forest tent caterpillars happen every decade or so and numbers remain high for a couple of years. Unlike eastern tent caterpillars, which build tents of webbing for protection, forest tent caterpillars form masses on tree trunks when they are not actively feeding. A huge cluster of writhing caterpillars is not a pleasant sight.

AS SPRING FADES into June in the forests of the southern Appalachians, the whites and pinks of the understory rhododendrons step onto center stage.

Summer heat begins to settle over the forest canopy, and hikers are not the only ones who look exhausted. The trees also seem to be feeling the effects. And indeed, they are. Beeches, oaks, and other trees are already gradually preparing themselves for their winter sleep. Thanks to photosynthesis, the storerooms under their bark and in their roots have been filled and they don't have much more to do to ensure a good start next spring. Their leaves, disposable sun catchers designed to last just a single season, are starting to look pretty beaten up. They show signs of damage by insects such as the beech leaf miner. This little beetle lays its eggs on beech leaves, where the larvae excavate meandering tunnels as they feed. These tracks turn brown, so that from a distance a heavily infested tree looks olive-colored instead of bright green. The adult beetles continue eating the larvae-damaged leaves, chewing holes until the leaves look as if someone has taken pot shots at them with a miniature shotgun.

Up until the beginning of July, it's relatively easy to peel off the cambium from spruce trees. After that, these trees start slowly pulling their sap out of this tissue, and the cambium becomes hard and woody. You can see the same thing happening with the trees' leaves and needles. They lose their soft green color and turn yellowish, as though they had lost their energy and are feeling weary.

High summer heat sometimes intensifies this effect. If there's not much precipitation, many trees jettison some of their leaves. The birch trees around our house often do this at the end of July and then hold on to their remaining solar panels until October. Cherries and mountain ash have often absorbed so much sunshine by August and made so much sugar from it that the trees close up shop, their foliage turns red, and their metabolism ticks over until the following spring.

Even the birds in the forest seem to be gradually running out of steam. You rarely hear the trills of songbirds or the drumming of woodpeckers. There are no urgent messages to convey, because many forest birds raise only one brood a year. The array of food on offer, such as insects or berries, is strictly seasonal and by late summer there are fewer options to choose from. It might surprise you to hear that. Many flowering plants are still at their peak and there are plenty of insects around. Blackberry bushes drip with berries. Surely this abundance would sustain another set of chicks.

This richness, however, is typical of prairie landscapes, both those designed by nature and those we humans create with our fields and landscaped areas. Summer continues in full swing in these open spaces, whereas forests are already preparing themselves for winter. Aphids, which sucked up fresh plant juices by the billion earlier in the year, are scarce. And many beetle and fly larvae assumed their adult forms weeks ago. Now, as the shadows of the trees lengthen, those adults prepare to sleep the winter away tucked under loose bark or in the leaf litter on the forest floor. It's little wonder the birds can no longer feast, and there simply aren't enough calories in the forest to support a second brood.

That's why the late-summer forest is relatively quiet and why, when I lead tours at this time of year, I'm often asked why Hümmel has so few birds. Paradoxically, things are quite different in the areas that have been clear-cut. Here, the landscape resembles more closely what you'd find in an open, grassy area. When all the trees have been cut down, magnificent stands of foxgloves, fireweed, and wild roses move in. With their three-foot-high arrays of red and pink flowers, they attract bees and other nectar-seeking insects. In places like this, songbirds can still find a wide variety of food and therefore often manage to produce up to three broods a season. And you can hear them singing all that time.

SUMMER CANNOT LAST forever, and the time comes when the trees lose their leaves. The sky turns gray and cold rain drips from the branches. Who wants to hike in the forest in weather like that? And yet, it can be rewarding if you know what to look for. Thin silty layers of earth either on or near trails are often most revealing. Hooves and paws leave imprints like a seal in wax. And if you know the day the last heavy rain fell, you can roughly estimate how much time has passed since an animal went by. A downpour will either wash the tracks away or, at the very least, blur their outlines so you can barely make them out. So, if the last time it rained was the day before yesterday and you notice a neat, sharp outline of a deer hoof, you know the animal was here no more than a couple of days ago.

There's a reason rain is called liquid sunshine. The forest cannot do without moisture. In many places, it doesn't rain nearly enough in the summer. Or perhaps I should say the trees drink too much. On a hot day, a mature tree sucks up to 130 U.S. gallons (500 liters) of water from the ground. Even severe summer storms don't recharge the forest's underground supply of water enough to satisfy these thirsty giants. Therefore, trees in the forest need to stock up on water, and they do this in fall and winter. When it rains for days on end, it might make you feel better to think how the dreary deluge is working to fill the trees' reservoirs. A single tree can store more than 6,500 U.S. gallons (25,000 liters) of water in the tiniest of pores in the soil around its roots. As long as the soil has not been compacted, for example by machines, the excess from weeks-long rains (that is, the portion that escapes being sucked up by the trees) slowly finds its way deep down into the groundwater supply, a process that can take many decades.

FALL IS MUSHROOM time in the forest. You can usually find the first wave in late summer when heavy rain soaks the ground after a long, dry period. But those are the impatient ones that can't quite wait until the official start of the season, which is in the fall after the first prolonged periods of rain. The fruiting bodies of most edible forest fungi are formed, indirectly, from the sugars produced by the trees, and the trees must deliver it in sufficiently large quantities to satisfy the fungi's demands for payment for their services. In the spring and summer, the trees use most of their sugar to grow their leaves, branches, and fruit. By late summer, however, most trees have stored enough sugar to see them through the winter and the following spring. This means they can pass an increasing portion of their production along to their partners on the forest floor. The fungi, anticipating their annual bonus, get busy with the task of reproduction and growing the delicious mushrooms you can then gather. Also, the damp fall is a much better time for reproduction because the mushroom caps stay intact longer than in the heat of summer. It's not just people who enjoy eating the fungi's fruiting bodies. Animals from big bears to small slugs enjoy them, too.

The exception to this fall abundance is the much-sought-after morel, which springs up in its largest numbers in the spring after a forest fire has cleared an area. The mushrooms make the most of the sun pouring into the space and the concentration of nutrients in the wood ash. Mushroom hunters come from far and wide to collect these delicacies.

Fall is also the time of year pigs go hog wild on oil- and carbohydrate-rich nuts—if they are available. Some years, oaks and beeches provide these in enormous quantities, and in those years both feral pigs and deer eat their fill. The animals quickly stock up on those all-important calories so they can build up a layer of fat under their skin. When the cold of winter hits, deer dial their metabolisms down a couple of notches and spend their days dozing in thickets, where they can lie covered in a coating of snow, unseen by predators and protected from the wind. Feral pigs find shelter also, and in Canada they have been known to dig tunnels in the snow—so-called pigloos—where they can take advantage of snow's insulating properties to keep the winter chill away.

You might even be able to watch as mice, squirrels, and jays stash their portion of the harvest safely in underground pantries. A single jay can easily find up to ten thousand of these, but squirrels sometimes seem to lose track and mice do not always make it through the winter. The following spring, bunches of saplings burst from these forgotten hiding places.

~ 13 ~

Hidden Connections

LET'S TAKE A step back—or perhaps you might say a step closer—and consider the relationships playing out in the forest. Nature is complicated. To understand how populations of predators and prey affect each other, we can look to Isle Royale, an island in Lake Superior in the state of Michigan. Here, Nature started a unique experiment, one that researchers have been observing since 1958. First, moose arrived on the island over the frozen lake. The lake thawed, the moose were stranded, and their population exploded. They ate their way through the underbrush and destroyed most of the young trees. Then, during another harsh winter, a wolf pack settled on the island and set about reducing the moose population. The remoteness of the island was a gift for the researchers. With both populations more or less trapped, they could study the interaction in a relatively small area (more than two hundred square miles / five hundred square kilometers, but still).

The researchers expected that if the number of wolves rose, moose numbers would fall because the wolves would catch and eat more of them. Eventually, wolf numbers would fall because it would take the wolves longer to find the moose and hunt them down, so more wolves would starve. Moose numbers would then start to rise. But you could look at this dynamic completely differently. When the moose have a lot to eat, they reproduce so the wolves have lots of moose to catch. The more moose are killed by wolves, the more the wolves reproduce. And yet, a larger population of wolves means more stress on the predators because they must now put more energy into defending their territories from other wolves. The fluctuations in the moose population, therefore, depend more on the condition of their habitat than on the presence of wolves—unless a particularly harsh winter comes along. In a harsh winter, food becomes so scarce that many moose die of starvation. If the wolves now hunt the remaining animals more vigorously, it can cause the moose population to collapse. Are you completely confused? I'm not surprised. I'm describing this to you to show that interdependencies in nature are often not as obvious as we once thought.

Perhaps the connections will be easier to understand if we pay less attention to the fluctuations in the size of the herbivore population and more on the changes in their behavior. And to do that, we'll travel in our minds to Yellowstone National Park. There, too, there were way too many herbivores (mostly elk). These large deer drastically reduced tree cover until they'd stripped extensive areas of the landscape bare. Park rangers exacerbated the problem by feeding the elk in winter, which allowed the herds to continue increasing in size. The turning point came in 1995, when the rangers, together with scientists, released wolves into the park. By 1996, rangers had introduced a total of thirty-one animals. The wolves set about steadily increasing their numbers and did one thing above all others: they ate elk. So, the number of elk declined steadily from 1995 (16,791) to 2004 (8,335) to settle at a lower level. The number of wolves rose to 174 in 2003 before declining to a sustainable level of about 100.

But more important than the decline in the number of herbivores was the change in their behavior. In earlier times, the elk had enjoyed browsing along the riverbanks, destroying the vegetation that protected the river from erosion. Rivers and streams began to cut into the land and carry off valuable soil. The sediment in the water affected fish and other aquatic organisms, and in some places the park became little more than an elk zoo. With the return of the wolves, elk began to avoid the riverbanks, where they were particularly easy prey. Shrubs and trees soon began to grow once again and line the banks. Now beavers came back as well, because they had access to the trees they used to build their dams and the branches they relied on for food. The rivers began to meander through the valleys once again. The bends slowed the rate at which the water flowed and therefore the rate at which the water eroded the banks. All this happened thanks to the reintroduction of a top predator.

The balances in nature are not simply predator and prey but include ripple effects that affect plants and creatures large and small, and the landscape itself. Here's an example you might see in your own backyard. Say you are watching a caterpillar eating leaves on your favorite tree. A bird eats the caterpillar and you are happy because the bird has been fed and the caterpillar is gone. But thinking back to my earlier mention of the trees in the forest summoning help, another beneficial insect could have already been on the job: a predatory wasp might have laid its eggs inside the caterpillar

Pileated woodpecker activity, Letchworth State Park, New York

and the bird intercepted its attack. Here, we have a cascade of interactions: leaf, caterpillar, wasp, bird. To keep the forest healthy, we need to look beyond partnerships to what biologists are now calling guilds—arrangements of give-and-take that involve different winners and losers depending on the day or season but together keep the whole system running smoothly.

Even elements we think of as destructive have their place. Take the spruce budworm in Pacific Northwest forests. Thirteen species of ant eat the budworms. Twenty-seven species of birds, including pileated woodpeckers, feast on the budworms and the ants. The woodpeckers need homes and budworm outbreaks lead to dead trees in the forest. Dead trees become hollow snags where pileated woodpeckers excavate cavities for their nests. When the snags fall over, they become logs rotting on the forest floor that ants use as nesting spaces. Pileated woodpeckers shred the logs to get at the ants. Meanwhile, the ants climb up into the crowns of trees in search of spruce budworms. The woodpeckers join them. Once in a while, the budworm supply exceeds demand and the population explodes. More budworms mean more snags so more woodpeckers can move in. More snags also mean more rotting logs, which mean more ants, and so between them the woodpeckers and the ants get the outbreak under control. And along the way, woodpecker cavities become homes for other forest birds, mammals, and insects, and the rotting wood of downed snags returns nutrients to the soil.

Sometimes we can see what's happening but we don't yet know exactly what is going on or what effect the process has on the forest as a whole. Take holly trees growing in East Coast forests. Hollies produce red berries to entice birds to eat them so the birds can scatter the hollies' seeds to other parts of the forest. But not all the berries turn red. Some stay green. Little midges grow in the green berries, and the midges do not want the birds to eat them. The birds overlook the green berries and the midges overwinter in their cozy homes, emerging in their flying form in the spring. The adult midges mate, and the females lay their eggs in the flowers of the holly trees. But the females also inject holly flowers with a fungus. The fungus has been found only in holly berries containing midge larvae, and the midge larvae have been found only in holly berries. If you find green berries hidden among the red berries on hollies, there could well be midge larvae inside with their fungal companions living out a cycle that so far remains a mystery.

The forest is full of these fascinating interconnections. You might like to use a small portion of a forest near you to conduct some up-close-and-personal observations of what is going on. You never know what you might find. For instance, in the forestlands near Jane's house, an observer recently spotted, and wrote a scientific paper on, a dragon-fly behavior that had never been noticed before. He called it the spin-dry cycle, which is when dragonflies fly in a spiral pattern to dry off after dipping themselves into the water to wash (a behavior he calls splash-dunk).

You can record your observations on an increasing number of citizen science websites. Who knows what marvels we will discover in the forest if people pool their resources and share what they have found?

~ 14 ~

Spotting
Wildlife

ONE OF THE attractions forests have for us is that we hope to catch sight of some of the wildlife involved in these complex interactions. You can go on foot, of course, but other dependable and even romantic modes of transportation can enhance your wildlife viewing: you can make your observations from the back of a horse, a canoe or kayak, or even the comfort of your own car.

I know horses are quite large, and I admit there was a time when I was afraid of them. One kick from a hoof is all it takes to break a leg, even a strong one. But over time I learned to get along well with horses, mostly because we've owned a couple of them for some years. I never wanted to ride one, but in the early 1990s my wife got her wish to own a horse. The second one, which we acquired only so that the one we had bought for riding wouldn't be all alone, turned out to want attention, too. And so, I conquered my fear and learned to ride on Bridgi (as the new young mare was called). And I can attest that when the forest is viewed from this elevated position, small though the difference is, it looks quite different. As a bonus, wildlife such as deer are less likely to run away when they see you on horseback. Horses are, after all, herbivores, and therefore deer don't regard them as a threat. Just like out in the Serengeti, the animals are not much concerned by other animals of a similar type, and the deer go about their business as normal. A person sitting on top of this peaceful animal is clearly thought of as part of the horse.

If you're not a horse person, kayaking makes for a wonderfully peaceful way to view wildlife. In a boat, you're not trampling sensitive habitat and you can paddle to places impossible to reach on foot. The U.S. is filled with rivers designated as "wild" and "scenic," many of which flow through forested areas. But be sure not to disturb sensitive areas just because you can reach them. Nesting birds (and alligators!) need their privacy.

It sounds odd, but you can also increase your chances of seeing wildlife if you watch from a car. You might have noticed this already. Because deer and other animals don't recognize cars as threats, they are happy to browse along the edges of highways and country roads. You are sitting lower down in a car than when riding a horse, but on the plus side you are more protected from the weather—and from the wildlife, if it is large. Moose, when encountered up close, can deliver deadly kicks and are better viewed from the safety of your vehicle. Cars can also provide particularly good places from which to spot black bears that either need to cross the road or are drawn to the wildflowers that proliferate along roadside edges. Jane has seen a few black bears on wilderness hikes, but she's also had some sightings along highways. Black bears, despite the common name, are not always black, especially in western North America. Jane's favorite sighting was of a small, cinnamon-colored black bear munching on dandelions along a park road in northern Saskatchewan.

You can, of course, also see animals when you are out walking. However, because hunters target them, prey animals such as deer are often extremely wary. A few times a year, however, deer, in particular, are less guarded. The first is mating season. At this time of year, they can't think straight because of the hormones coursing through their systems and they become less cautious—particularly the males. The rutting season often draws wildlife watchers as the animals are highly visible even in areas with heavy hunting. In places where the deer are extremely active, such as an area close to where I live in Hümmel, you can set up a folding chair on the side of the road for a couple of weeks to observe love-crazed males bellowing and rounding up their harems. Just make sure to keep to the speed limit at this time of year to avoid collisions. The second good time to spot wildlife is after hunting season closes. When the guns fall silent, word soon gets around among the wild animals.

The further the last shot recedes into the past, the more the animals forget their fear, which makes just before hunting season starts up again one of the best times to go out deer spotting. At this time of year, deer, peacefully grazing in meadows and along forest edge lands, will take little notice of you hiking as long as you keep your distance. (About the length of one football field is good.)

With most large animals, you are more likely to spot signs of their presence than the animals themselves. Trotter tracks, droppings, and shelters are just a few of the clues that feral hogs are in the area. They also leave distinctive wallows. After a refreshing bath in the mud (where you can sometimes still make out the pig's outline), they rub themselves up against trees they select specifically for this purpose. Rubbing removes both dried mud and porcine bristles, which catch on the rough bark. The vegetation along the trails to these trees is dotted with the dirt that drips off the wet animals, muddy calling cards that show feral hogs have walked this way. Pigs are not the only animals to post signs on trees. Bears also like a good scratch on rough bark to remove their winter coat, and bucks can do a spectacular amount of damage when they use low-hanging branches to remove the velvet on their antlers when it starts to itch.

Many animals attack bark for its tasty inner layer, which is most accessible when the trees' sap is running in the spring. At this time of year animals are hungry and have few menu options. Porcupines climb to a comfortable spot to sit while they gnaw. Deer, elk, and moose nibble as high as they can reach. Black bears stand tall and strip bark up high, and squirrels scamper all over the place.

Deer, moose, and bears also leave messages in trees for others of their kind, such as "This Is My Territory, Stay Away" or "Lonely and Seeking a Mate," gnawing, clawing, and, in the case of bears, rubbing vigorously to impregnate the bark with their scent. When you see how high the marks are, whether they have been made by teeth or claws, and if there's any hair stuck to them, you get a good idea of who left them.

There's another sign bears might be around: bears' nests. Bears shred bark and use it as bedding, but the bears' nests I'm talking about are high up in the trees. In places such as Algonquin Provincial Park in Canada, hungry black bears climb beech trees in search of nutritious beechnuts, leaving claw marks on the trunks as they climb. Bears are nimble, but not particularly tidy. They wedge themselves in a convenient crotch and bend branches toward them so they can reach the nuts dangling from the tips. Once in a while, a branch breaks and gets caught in the bear's perch. When the bear has eaten its fill and climbs back down, it can leave an accumulation of debris that looks something like an untidy eagle's nest.

Finding wolf tracks anywhere other than remote places in the Northwest and the North is unlikely, but that makes spotting signs of these elusive creatures particularly exciting. The one place in the East where you might at least hear wolves is Algonquin Provincial Park in Canada, where the park rangers schedule public howls in August and September. Sometimes, if you're lucky, the wolves howl back.

The first time I came across wolf tracks was when I saw them imprinted in dried mud along a trail in Sweden. I was traveling with my family along the border with Norway— by canoe. A canoe and wolf tracks? How does that work? As the canoe trip was along a series of lakes, sometimes we had to portage. We unpacked the canoe, lifted it out of the water, and attached it to a two-wheeled trolley. Then we repacked it and battled our way for miles along faint forest trails across the undulating landscape. The whole exhausting process kept our weary eyes fixed on the ground. Once in a while, we had to stop and catch our breath, which allowed us to spot the very first wolf tracks we had ever seen. There were no hikers in this remote area, and, at the time, Sweden's largest wolf population lived there. We felt amply rewarded and pushed our canoe with renewed energy toward the next lake.

Why did I mention hikers? Because they often bring their dogs with them, which can make it tricky to spot wolf tracks. Dogs and wolves are closely related, and their paw prints are very similar. Even I can hardly tell the difference between the track of a large dog and the track of a wolf. A few resources can help, and the most important of these are news reports. Because wolves attract everyone's attention, a wolf sighting is reported immediately, and the news comes out the next day. If you think you see wolf tracks in an area with no confirmed wolf sightings, the tracks probably belong to the wolf's domesticated counterpart. In wolf territory, however, it's worth taking a closer look.

Wolves move differently from dogs. Their paw prints will be arranged in an almost completely straight line, with the prints from the right and left paws only slightly offset, and the prints from the back paws almost directly tracking the prints from the front paws. To be sure, look to the right and left of the track: in wet weather, if the track comes from a dog, you should also be able to see a track made by its owner. Wolf and coyote tracks look similar, but wolf tracks are about four inches (ten centimeters) wide by five inches (twelve centimeters) long, while coyote tracks are much smaller, about two inches by two-and-half inches (five centimeters by six centimeters).

It's easier to tell whether the tracks come from a dog, a wolf, or a coyote if you also find scat. Most pets eat canned or dried food, which means the piles they leave tend to be one shade of brown with a uniform texture. With wolf scat, you can usually tell what animals it's been eating. Bits of bone are mixed with animal hair. Coyote scat is much like wolf scat but slightly smaller and shinier and it usually contains rodent or rabbit hair and much smaller bone fragments. If you're not sure, you can always collect some of the scat in a plastic bag and send it off to a wolf expert for analysis.

Does all this mean it is dangerous to go out in the forest? If one day you're lucky enough to find yourself face-to-face with a wolf, I guarantee your heart will start racing. It can't hurt to pass along a couple of pieces of advice just in case. Make yourself as large as possible, clap your hands, and yell. That will make the wolf aware of your presence. Look the animal directly in the eye. If you don't feel safe, retreat slowly, with the emphasis on slowly. Running can trigger a predator chase response. Don't throw sticks or stones at the animal, because that will only make it want to investigate. For extra safety, carry pepper spray. You don't have to take any other precautions. Wolves are just curious and are unlikely to attack. Mostly you'll only catch sight of them in the distance before they disappear.

You've hit the jackpot if you're lucky enough to find wolf tracks, but finding fox tracks is a good consolation prize. You can learn to spot the difference between fox tracks and the prints left by small dogs because a fox moves through the landscape like its larger, wilder brother, leaving behind a long, straight line of paw prints. The central pad is set back from the toe pads, making the prints longer and narrower than the slightly more rounded paw prints of a dog.

If foxes are around, there's a good chance a den is nearby. You won't find them right by trails, but if you are wandering through the underbrush in search of mushrooms, you might come across one of these holes in the ground. Usually they have multiple entrances and exits dug under a cover of bushes. If they are in use, you will find fresh scratch marks with nothing growing out of the freshly dug earth.

North America is also home to wildcats: mountain lion, lynx, and bobcat. Your best chance of seeing one of these is probably on webcams set up to record animals passing in the night. They can be surprisingly close and yet invisible to you. The prints of all three are similar, differing mostly in size. If you draw a mental line down the middle of wolf or dog tracks (down the middle toe), the two sides are mirror images of each other. Cat tracks are asymmetrical. Also, you rarely see claw marks on the prints of big cats, because they retract them to keep them sharp. The claws of wolves and other canines, in contrast, usually leave depressions in the soft earth. Mountain lions tend to move in straight lines, often toward trees, which they climb, whereas lynx and bobcats often meander.

Many other animals might be perching in the trees above you: raccoons, possums, and porcupines, to say nothing of squirrels. When you think of squirrels, the eastern gray probably comes to mind, but tucked away in the forests of North America are Douglas squirrels, flying squirrels, red squirrels, black squirrels, and fox squirrels.

Found in southern pine savannahs, fox squirrels live in a three-way relationship with longleaf pines and fungi, one of those guilds we talked about that benefits each participant. The fungi live off sugars produced by the pines in exchange for providing communication and catering services for the trees. In spring, when the pines' seeds are most viable, fox squirrels break into the pines' green cones, making quite a racket. If you hear the sounds of demolition and see shredded cones flying, look up to see if a fox squirrel is at work. Fox squirrels are the only squirrels strong enough to break apart the pines' tough cones and fast enough to evade predators as they run from tree to tree. The squirrels also eat the fruiting bodies of the fungi, and so fox squirrels distribute both the pines' seeds and the fungi the pines need to grow well. The squirrels retreat to nearby stands of trees with closed canopies to build their nests and raise their young. From there it's a hop, skip, and a jump to the open stands of pines for food.

If you hear a scolding sound from high up in a Douglas fir in the Pacific Northwest, you might be intruding into the territory of a tiny but feisty Douglas squirrel warning everything within earshot that you are thundering along the trail disrupting the ways of the forest. They don't throw things at you intentionally, but if you walk under trees when they're collecting cones for snacks, the cones can come tumbling down from an alarming height and cause you to step aside for fear of one landing on your head. It's easy to mistake their piercing shrieks for a bird call. If no cones come raining down, stop and look around to see if you can spot the little town crier. If you do, it will probably immediately scuttle to the other side of the tree trunk to hide itself from view.

The way squirrels indicate alarm, either by the sounds they make or how they twitch their tails, is fascinating. Scientists at the University of Miami are investigating a variety of calls and tail twitches in gray squirrels that seem to distinguish between aerial and terrestrial predators. Some seem aimed at the predators themselves to let them know they've been spotted. Others seem aimed at their fellow squirrels to let them know now would be a good time to make themselves scarce. Stop for a while and see if you can figure out if the squirrel is communicating directly with you ("Go away! I've spotted you!") or with others of its kind ("Watch out! Human on the loose!").

In many places, chipmunks might join you on your hike for lunch, hoping for a handout. They are endearing, energetic little creatures small enough to fit into your travel coffee mug. No matter how appealing they might be, resist the temptation to feed them. There's plenty of healthy food in the forest for them to snack on.

Opossums, usually referred to simply as possums, are the only marsupials in North America. When stressed, they keel over and play dead, whether they want to or not. Not only do they look dead, they also smell dead, which probably helps keep the foxes and bobcats away. They do a good job of cleaning up some of the forest inhabitants we consider less than desirable. Immune to snake venom, they are happy to snack on snakes. They lack sweat glands, so they groom themselves frequently to cool down. This gives them the opportunity to pick off and eat any ticks they have accumulated, thereby removing a large number of them from the forest, which is a good thing. Another good thing about possums is that they rarely get rabies because their low body temperatures make them inhospitable hosts for the virus. So, possums may not be the most loveable forest animals to look at, but they are your forest friends.

Raccoons, in contrast, with their bandit-like masks and dexterous paws, look adorable. You can find them patting the bottoms of streams and wetlands looking for crayfish to crunch down or frogs to munch. Their front paws are exquisitely sensitive to touch—especially in water, because the protective horny layer that covers them becomes flexible when wet. They also have tiny hairs above their claws that help them identify objects before they grasp them. Unfortunately, unlike possums, they have been known to carry rabies.

Where there are live animals, there are also dead ones, and a small scene at my forest lodge reminded me that they also belong in this book. One day I was sitting on the sofa during my lunch break. As I took a bite out of my cheese sandwich I glanced outside and saw snowflakes. They were floating softly to the ground—too softly. When I took a closer look, I saw they were not snowflakes but downy feathers. I stood up and went over to the window. It immediately became clear where the feathers were coming from. A jay was happily plucking a great tit so it could get to the meat inside.

Small tragedies such as this happen often under the leafy covering of the trees. A number of predators hunt birds out there. I can think of squirrels, martens, and foxes, to name just a few of the mammals. Among birds, there are the corvids (magpies, jays, crows, and ravens) and various species of owl (barred owls and great horned owls, for instance). Then there are nimble raptors such as Cooper's hawks and sparrowhawks with short wings so they can fly through tight spaces and long tails that act like rudders to steer them through the trees.

You might find a pile of feathers on top of a tree stump. Like humans, animals, it seems, find tables convenient when there is some butchering to be done. You won't be able to tell exactly which species was at work here, but you will be able to tell whether it was a mammal or a bird. The latter have no teeth, so whereas a fox, for example, bites off tough feathers, raptors rip them out whole. You can often find a nick or a kink on the shaft where the bird got a firm hold on the feather with its beak.

For birds that are not equipped to hunt anything much larger than insects or perhaps the occasional frog, trees make giant food depots if only they can find a way to breach their defenses. If you see a neat row of holes punched through a tree's bark, you are looking at the work of a type of woodpecker called a sapsucker. The bird drills through the bark to get at the tree's sugary sap flowing in the vessels beneath. Sugar-loving hummingbirds, wasps, and butter-flies, none of which have the tools to drill down to the sap themselves, are all drawn to the bird's handiwork (or, per-haps I should say, beak work). Sapsuckers sometimes snack on the insects that collect around their sap wells. You might wonder how hummingbirds, which are attracted to red flowers, find the sapsuckers' holes. Might it be the red patch on the sapsuckers' heads that alerts the tiny birds that sugar is there for the taking?

If you come across larger round holes pecked out of trees so deep you can see the light-colored wood beneath the bark, you are looking at the excavations made by the smaller woodpeckers, downys or hairys for instance, as they search for insects. Larger, rectangular holes with wood chips on the ground below are evidence that pileated woodpeckers have been pecking at the tree. Pileated woodpeckers, the larg-est woodpeckers in North America, can remove enormous chunks of wood. Jane has seen examples in forests where she lives that look as though beavers have climbed up trees and chomped through the trunks. She was slightly nervous, therefore, when one day while working on this book, she caught a pileated woodpecker checking out the wooden sid-ing on her house. Thankfully it didn't find her office wall a fruitful spot to start excavations, and it moved on.

One very special case of woodpecker activity in North America is the red-cockaded woodpecker. This woodpecker is endangered and forests in the South are being managed to provide it with more habitat. Red-cockaded woodpeckers need longleaf pines with heartrot—that is, pines at least 150 years old that have begun to decay from the inside out. In the normal course of events, pines are cut down when they are much younger than this and so the birds' habitat has been shrinking.

Wood-boring beetle activity, Algonquin Provincial Park, Ontario

If you are in the South and lucky enough to see pines with largish holes dripping sap, you may be looking at trees where red-cockaded woodpeckers are or have recently been nesting. Foresters mark these trees with white bands, so they know to protect them. The birds need trees with heart-rot so they can excavate nesting cavities in them, but they also need trees that are still alive so they will drip sap from the small holes the woodpeckers drill under their nest cavities. The sap from these wells is the red-cockaded woodpeckers' home-security system, trapping rat snakes that sneak up the trunk to eat their babies.

After a forty-year absence, in summer 2019, red-cockaded woodpeckers were nesting once again in Sumter National Forest in South Carolina thanks to habitat-restoration work by federal, state, and local organizations. Scientists are tracking the birds using a new style of leg band that can be scanned with a device that works a bit like a grocery-store scanner.

Woodpeckers also drill into trees for insects. The trees with the best selection of insects are usually already dead or at least so severely ill that their end is near. In summer, when bark beetle populations boom, the presence of wood-peckers indicates which trees are suffering from a beetle attack. Wherever juicy white larvae (the beetle's offspring) are spreading out under the bark, the birds hack and poke around until they've caught most of the tasty treats. Large sections of bark fall off during this feast. If you catch sight of large patches of light wood where bark should be, you know beetles have targeted the tree. The missing patches of bark are so large that they are clearly visible even from a distance.

The woodpeckers' interest in trees doesn't stop there. They are also attracted by dead trunks slowly rotting away in the low light of the forest floor. Thousands of species of insects lay their eggs here. The pale larvae often spend years eating their way through the crumbling wood before they pupate and finally experience the world for a few short weeks as beetles. You can see these "woodpecker pantries" particularly well in winter. The busy bustling of ants has stopped, and flying insects are sleeping their way through the cold season, hidden under loose patches of bark. In these lean times, woodpeckers turn to the dead trunks and hack long slivers of light-colored wood out of them. Deep inside, they find the protein-rich larvae they seek, the reward for all their hard work. In places with lots of larvae, you will find the ground covered with dead wood that has been hacked to pieces.

Then there are less dramatic signs of animal activity. In spring, beechnuts sprout in old stands of beeches. The unfurling cotyledons of the tiny seedlings make the baby trees look like tiny butterflies cautiously spreading their wings. Sometimes a whole bunch of them come up from the same spot in the ground. But how can that be? Beechnuts are heavy and fall directly at the feet of the mother trees no matter which way the wind blows. Theoretically, they should sprout in an evenly spaced pattern around the base of the trunk. Okay, perhaps two or three might end up on the same spot, but ten or more? When that happens, chance has nothing to do with it. Squirrels—or, more often, mice— are the unwitting forest gardeners here. In fall, they stashed their winter supplies of food, so they could feast on the oil-rich seeds under a protective cover of snow.

The bunch of seedlings is a testament to a small drama that played out on the forest floor. Clearly, the previous winter a hungry fox or coyote came by and made a meal of the hardworking little mouse. Deprived of their guardian, the provisions the little rodent so carefully tucked away were left abandoned in the ground to sprout the following spring. Depending on your point of view, you could frame the story somewhat differently: the fox freed the tree embryos from their captor and so ensured their survival.

Before we leave this chapter, I should put in a word about taking care around wildlife. It's always a thrill to see wild animals, but it's easy to get carried away and forget that they are just that—wild—and want to get too close to them or on the other end of the scale, to feel so nervous about them that it spoils your appreciation of wild spaces. Each place you visit will have more information about animals you might encounter and what to do if you meet them.

The goal on most hikes is not to meet wild animals in the first place. Traveling in groups and making noise will alert them to your presence so they have time to move away. If you do spot a potentially dangerous animal, this is not the time to be taking selfies to show your friends back home. Back away to let the animal know you are not a threat, but move slowly to avoid suggesting you are potential prey. You are the visitor and allowing animals their personal space and privacy is the most important rule for a respectful, and safe, visit.

~ 15 ~

Finding Beauty in Small Things

NOT ALL FOREST hikes yield wildlife sightings, and I'll admit it can get a bit monotonous if all you see are trees. If you don't see any animals, sooner or later, even the most exciting search begins to lose its appeal. There's an iron-clad rule here: the larger the animal, the rarer the sighting. There are two reasons for this. Larger animals need larger territories and carnivores need more space than herbivores. A lynx will prowl over a territory of twenty square miles (fifty square kilometers), whereas a fox needs less than half a square mile (one square kilometer) of land to call its own, and a deer manages with a small fraction of that. It's the same for small animals, but on a greatly reduced scale. So maybe it's time to switch focus to the world at our feet.

In roughly ten square feet (one square meter) of an undisturbed forest, there can be as many as one hundred spiders jostling for space to catch their prey. This means that when you stretch out on a nice, soft layer of fallen leaves, many eyes will be watching you. Spiders are after flies, sow bugs, springtails, mites, and other spiders, all of which are rummaging around under the leaves in even greater numbers than the spiders hunting them. If you want to be sure of a wildlife sighting, all you have to do is squat down and concentrate on a small patch of forest floor. A sand sieve (the kind you can buy in a toy shop) and a magnifying glass will serve you well if you decide to set out on an expedition into the microcosmos. A lens of about 16x magnification works well—either one you can hold in your hand or one you can attach to your mobile phone. If you have a picnic blanket to lie on while you're at it, so much the better. You'll be able to watch for longer and enjoy your discoveries that much more.

Expeditions like this are more interesting if you can identify the animals bustling around you. Because there are so many of them, my advice is to concentrate on just one class of animal and bring along a field guide for the group you've chosen to focus on. Let's stay with spiders for the moment. The spiders you're most likely to run into in the forest—and I mean this literally—are the ones that spin their webs across the trails. When Jane visited Congaree National Park in South Carolina, there were posters up about banana spiders (also known as golden silk orb weavers)—not because they're dangerous but because they look as though they should be: large, yellow, and everywhere. In fact, banana spiders bite only when pinched or squeezed and, unless you are allergic to their bites, the most you need to worry about is walking into one of their impressively large webs.

If you take a moment to look at them up close, spiders can be incredibly beautiful and because they often hang out motionless in the middle of their webs, they make good subjects for photographs. Jane has a photograph, taken on

Orb weaver, Anacortes, Washington

the deck of her home next to the forest, of an orb-weaver spider with striking blue underparts that are only visible from close-up. So, if you can resist the impulse to turn away, try having a closer look. You might be entranced by what you see.

If you are feeling slightly more adventurous, you can also check out damp places for salamanders and other amphibians. Salamander larvae are another good indicator of water quality. Salamanders that lay their eggs in water need very clean streams if their larvae are to survive, which is one reason salamanders have become so rare in some places. Where I live in Germany, we regularly find adult salamanders, especially after an overnight rain. That's when they come out to hunt snails and other small creatures. On rainy evenings, when we come home late after visiting friends, we have to take special care when we walk up the path to our house to make sure we don't inadvertently step on any of these little critters.

If salamanders happen to visit you regularly, as they do us, or if you know of a place in the forest frequented by these amphibians, you might like to start a small photographic record of the salamanders you find. In some species individuals have unique color markings, which means you can recognize them year after year. And you can do this for a long time because salamanders live for decades. (They have been known to live up to fifty years in captivity.) So, you may find it worthwhile to create a photographic registry of "your" salamanders to help you identify old friends.

One of the best places to find salamanders is in the southern Appalachian Mountains. Indeed, this area has the highest diversity of salamanders in the world, partly because it was not covered in ice during the last ice age and salamanders here have had thousands of years to diversify, and partly because of the abundance of cool, moist forests, a favorite salamander habitat. In 2019, the Hickory Nut Gorge green salamander from North Carolina was described for science for the very first time. It has been developing as a separate species for ten to twelve million years, which predates the time the human lineage split off from the lineage that evolved into chimpanzees.

Before we look at a few specific salamanders, here are some fun salamander facts. Not all salamanders need streams as some spend all their life on land, but all of them need a moist environment with even temperatures. Because they live in moist places, some of them have dispensed with lungs and breathe through their skin instead. And, just one more thing: most salamanders are silent because they cannot hear. However, as they are slung low to the ground, they can pick up sound vibrations, "hearing" through their bodies in much the same way elephants can "hear" through their feet.

Red-backed salamanders are one of the Appalachians' lungless salamander species. The females lay their eggs in moist, rotting logs. These feisty salamanders are territorial and form monogamous pair bonds. They rarely stray more than a few yards from home, but if a female does happen to wander off and spend time in another male's territory, her mate can smell her betrayal and punishes her with threatening postures and little nips when she returns.

Olympic torrent salamanders, found only in the forests of the Olympic Peninsula in Washington State, have some lung capacity but mostly breathe through their skin. They live in mountain streams. If you stop by a waterfall, which is a wonderful thing to do as the air is particularly clean and invigorating in such spots, take a look to see if you can find any of these salamanders in the splash zone. They are brownish on top and yellowish underneath and up to four inches (ten centimeters) long. If, while you are there, you hear a sound rather like a creaking door, look around for a coastal giant salamander. It is much larger, up to twelve or thirteen inches (thirty to thirty-three centimeters) long, with a marbled patterning on its brownish or grayish skin. Along with the California giant salamander, it is one of the few salamanders to make any noise.

Salamanders are important indicators of water quality and to acknowledge this, the state of Pennsylvania has chosen the eastern hellbender—AKA the snot otter—as the state's official amphibian. Even longer than the giants on the West Coast, this nocturnal salamander grows up to two feet (sixty centimeters) in length. It is the third-largest salamander in the world, weighing up to five pounds (half a kilogram) and living up to fifty years. The color of mud and covered with a layer of mucus, it is one of the lungless salamanders. Snot otters are hard to spot because they live only in unpolluted streams, they hide under rocks, they are active only at night, and they are getting increasingly rare. If you want to find one, you will probably need a snorkel and mask. They live in fast-moving water, so don't get so absorbed in your observations that you float away downstream and be aware that it is illegal to touch them—although their appearance will likely discourage you from doing that.

On the subject of forest health, I'd also like to mention ants. I've already explained how ants help maintain healthy forest soil as they collect, eat, and excrete large quantities of prey and dead insects and concentrate the nutrients they contain in and around their ant hills. Ants are also ingenious. Wood ants have developed a sophisticated climate control system for their anthills. When it gets too cold inside, they crawl out to warm themselves up in the sun. Then the warmed-up ants crawl back inside and radiate their warmth inside. In winter, the ants remain deep inside their hill, where their most likely disturbance comes from woodpeckers and feral hogs searching for beetle larvae, which enjoy the warmth to be found there. When spring rolls around, the industrious ants haul in a supply of forest debris to repair the holes created by the intruders. Foresters value ants in the forest not only because their anthills are nutrient hotspots, but also because they feed on forest defoliators, such as tent caterpillars and the larvae of conifer sawflies and gypsy moths.

Ants travel through the forest using long "roads" that lead out from their anthills. They move obstacles off these mini-highways so they can travel more efficiently. If you're close to an anthill, you'll find it easy to spot these transport routes. The larger the mound, the farther the industrious little creatures roam, and the more distance you should keep between yourself and the anthill. European red wood ants, for example, which are also found in North American forests, are not dangerous but contact with them is very unpleasant. Unlike other species of ants, they don't have a stinger, so they defend themselves by biting. And to make their defense more effective, they spray formic acid when they bite. More than once, a wood ant has made its way from my shoe up the inside of my pant leg (while I was driving) and then bitten down hard into soft skin—ouch! To prevent this from happening to you, tuck your pant legs into your socks and, if you find yourself standing for a while near an anthill, jog on the spot. If you keep your feet moving, the little creatures usually jump off.

Now that you know how to protect yourself, feel free to observe a red ant mound up close if you wish. You can see how the ants crowd around the many entrances or warm themselves up in the morning sun close to the anthill and watch what they carry and how they do it. I love observing a colony at work. And for those of you who've never smelled formic acid, its pungency will surprise you. Gently touch a spot where there are lots of ants and hold your hand there for a couple of seconds. The ants will bend their abdomens forward between their legs and spray you. Then shake the ants off, put your hand up close to your nose, and smell it. The aroma is so strong it'll almost make your eyes water.

Carpenter ants, a common ant in some North American forests, don't build anthills; instead they move into trees with rotting wood. They don't eat the moist, mushy wood, but they do clear it out to create cozy spots for their broods to live in.

Up until now we've talked mostly about species you can see easily with your naked eye. That is deceptive because all too often not only the general public but also professionals use this as a yardstick by which to measure species diversity. We almost completely overlook the creatures so tiny that they escape our natural optical abilities. Unfortunately, that often comes with value judgments about the animals' relative worth. Eagles versus ground beetles, lynx versus springtails—it's easy to guess which will win in the battle for our sympathy.

Just recently, in the ancient woodlands around the village of Hümmel where I live, a weevil known as the scaly deadwood beetle, which sounds only a little worse than its Latin name *Trachodes hispidus*, was discovered. This is one peculiar little fellow. It has a trunk like an elephant and protruding scales along its back that make it look like it's sporting a Mohawk haircut. I call it the Mohawk beetle. It cannot fly and usually doesn't need to. As a typical primordial forest dweller, it lives in an ancient ecosystem that changes little over the centuries. When disturbed, it retracts its little legs and plays dead—after all, it can't fly away. Its brown coloring makes a fine camouflage against leaf litter or dead branches. Unfortunately, this means you won't notice it unless you know what you're looking for.

I find creatures like this really interesting, because their presence proves that some of the deciduous trees growing near my home are descended from trees that grew in the primeval forest. In contrast to most places in Europe—which have historically been cleared, plowed, and turned into pasture until our forebears allowed them to grow trees once again—around Hümmel we find undisturbed old soils in which the tiny little Mohawks feel right at home. Perhaps local naturalists should be offering professionally guided tours for beetle-watching instead of bird-watching: the shy little creatures deserve to be celebrated. I'm sure there are similar stories about tiny creatures in an ancient forest near you just waiting to be discovered.

~ 16 ~

A Walk on
the Wild Side

IMAGINE THE FOLLOWING scene. You've been wandering for hours in a dark forest and slowly but surely the time for lunch approaches. Suddenly you come across a small, grassy clearing warmed by the sun. Wouldn't this be a lovely place to take a break? It's the absence of trees that draws you to this spot. Does that mean we don't like forests after all, and what really speaks to us are imposing trees standing in solitary splendor? This might sound like an odd question for someone like me to ask, but it's an important one because the answer affects how we engage with nature.

From an evolutionary perspective, humans are creatures of the plains. We're ideally equipped for dry, hot climates. Walking upright means that only a small portion of our body is directed to the warmth of the sun, and without fur to contend with we can cool ourselves effectively using our sweat glands. These characteristics allowed our ancestors to hunt by chasing their prey until the animals overheated and collapsed. Our exceptional eyesight helped because we could spot prey from a long way off. That meant our senses of hearing and smell did not need to be so well developed.

In the forest, however, the abilities I've just mentioned are not always adaptive. In a place where sunshine rarely penetrates, a way to keep warm is more important than a system for cooling off. Woodland creatures are configured completely differently. Vision is not as important as large ears and a keen sense of smell. What use is it to scan your surroundings with a watchful eye if you can't see past the tree trunks a few yards in front of you? Amongst the trees, the only way you can be aware of enemies in time to save yourself is if you can smell them coming from hundreds of yards away and hear the snapping of twigs as they approach. And because members of a large group can easily lose contact with one another in the undergrowth, forest dwellers tend to be loners.

In forests, then, our ancestors encountered ecosystems that were only marginally suitable for humankind. As we know, they fended off the cold with blankets made from animal skins and fires, and they improved sightlines by clearing large areas of the forest. Clearings. So, people do not naturally enjoy living in the forest, and this becomes obvious if you look around at the landscapes we fashion for ourselves: they are perfectly recreated plains. When it comes down to it, wheat and barley (and in many cases today corn, as well) are nothing more than different types of grass, albeit particularly productive ones. Then we have fields for cows (animals of the plains) and here and there a few small stands of trees. That's what much of Central Europe looked like a couple of hundred years ago, and that was the pattern the first European settlers took with them when they sailed to North America in the 1600s. They associated deep, dark forests with scary stories and cautionary tales.

All that has changed today—or has it? Think back to the clearing I described at the beginning of this chapter, a place where just about anyone would feel at ease. The attraction of open spaces is also the reason it feels so good to hike up high to a rocky open area with scenic views. If the area is not too remote, you might even find a bench to sit on. If not, you can probably find a more-or-less comfortable rock where you can take a break to survey your surroundings. There you have it, a pleasant place to sit and relax—and such rest stops are extremely popular. Apparently, our primordial instincts are stronger than we give them credit for in a modern world where reason reigns. And so, our love of forests is perhaps based in something other than their innate attraction for humankind: they are the last halfway-intact ecosystems left near the places we call home.

We are attracted to these green leafy spaces and also slightly wary, and that is as it should be, because there are times when it's wise to avoid stepping into a forest. One of these times is when a strong wind is blowing because then tree branches, or even whole trees, might fall. California's coastal redwoods are among the tallest trees in the world. When a redwood called the Dyerville Giant fell and hit the ground in a storm in 1991, local seismographs picked up the shock waves. Although the trees in the forest where you are walking are likely not 370 feet (over 100 meters) tall, as this tree was, it is definitely a good idea to stay out of the forest in high winds.

It is, however, fascinating to observe a forest from afar during a windstorm. If you watch the treetops, you will see how each tree moves slightly differently when the wind hits it. Some right themselves as others begin to bend. This means that when one tree is bending over, the tree next to it is providing support. The whole forest moves, but each individual tree moves to its own rhythm, protecting its neighbors and making the forest strong in the face of the storm.

Jane lives across from community forestlands full of western red cedar, hemlock, and Douglas fir. When a storm blows through, the forest's movements are mesmerizing.

What should you do if you get caught in the forest during a storm? Of course, it's wisest not to go out into the forest when the forecast predicts a storm, but in case one surprises you, it's a good idea to have a plan. What about the old German folk saying, "Stay away from the oak and find a beech instead"? It comes from observations made by our forebears, who found traces of lightning strikes on oak trees but never on beeches. And if their observations are correct, it seems it would be a good idea to seek shelter under a beech rather than an oak, right?

But this supposed refuge is not as safe as it seems, because beeches, as it turns out, are not exempt from lightning strikes. Their bark is smooth and, in a downpour, raindrops coalesce to form a continuous sheet of water that cascades down the trunk toward the roots. Oaks, in contrast, have rough, deeply fissured bark. The water flowing down forms hundreds of tiny waterfalls as it descends the trunk, and the river of rainwater is broken up into many smaller streams as it makes its way earthward. Lightning seeks the path where electrical conductivity is most efficient, and because rainwater doesn't sheet down their trunks, oaks don't offer the most attractive option—at least not on the outside.

Beneath the bark, however, in the outer growth rings, water is flowing in the vessels that transport water from the roots to the crown. And this is where the lightning ends up. These tiny vessels, no thicker than a human hair, are not designed to withstand such pressure, and they burst. Sometimes the explosion caused by a lightning strike packs so much energy that nearby trees are impaled by shards of wood with knife-sharp points that fly out from the oak. Years later you can still see the scar in the bark of an oak that has been struck by lightning. It is known as a lightning channel, and people took this as proof that oaks were lightning magnets. In fact, all species have the same odds of being struck by lightning. The deciding factor is not the species but the height. So, if you do get caught in a storm, avoid mountain tops and don't seek shelter under trees that tower above the forest canopy.

You're more likely to get caught in regular rain than a thunderstorm. What do you do if a heavy shower dumps on you and you don't have either a raincoat or an umbrella handy? Then the question becomes which tree offers you the best shelter. In contrast to the folk wisdom concerning lightning, when it comes to protection from rain, different species vary widely. Deciduous trees stretch their branches up and out to catch rainwater, so it runs down their branches to their trunks and from there down to their roots. Oaks and beeches are specialized water gatherers, which makes it particularly unpleasant to stand under them when it rains. To make things even more miserable, long after the sun has reappeared, raindrops continue to drip from their leaves, leading to the saying, "It always rains twice under deciduous trees."

Conifers native to northern latitudes are very different. In Canada and the northern states, there is more than enough moisture to go around and so there's no pressing need for spruce and Douglas fir to gather water with their branches. What concerns them more is heavy snowfall. The weight of this wintery white can break off the crowns of trees. That's why the branches stretch out parallel to the ground and then bend down at the tips. If a great deal of snow falls, the tree need only lower its "arms" as the weight bearing down on them increases. This reduces the tree's surface area and the snow slips off. What happens, then, when it rains? A lot of water runs away from the trunk to fall from the tips of the branches. This means it's always especially dry under conifers, which is something you can use to your advantage during a rain shower. The closer you stand to the trunk of a tree such as a spruce, the drier you will be.

Sometimes it's not raining but it is still decidedly damp. Even in these conditions mild dangers can lurk. Calm, foggy conditions can be deceptive. You're walking under mighty old trees. Everything seems fine. Indeed, it all looks rather romantic, a bit like in a fairytale when dark trunks loom through veils of mist only to disappear again. The water vapor in the air deadens sound so you feel completely alone with nature. And yet, when the fog is particularly thick you hear the occasional "whomp." It's a dull thump as though a large something has just hit the forest floor. And this is exactly what has happened.

What you're hearing is the sound made by branches about as thick as your arm as they fall from the crowns of mighty deciduous trees. And yet there's no breeze. If a storm were raging, you wouldn't be surprised if a branch fell, but in such calm weather, you don't expect danger from above. The culprit is the high level of humidity in the air. Dead and rotten branches act like sponges sucking up the water droplets in the mist. Their stability has already been severely compromised by fungi, bacteria, and beetle larvae, tiny organisms that diligently eat away at the wood, transforming it into a soft pulp with the texture of cotton balls. The absorbed moisture is the proverbial last straw. (Or, as the German saying has it, "The drop that causes the barrel to overflow.") The additional weight is too much for the weakened wood to bear, and the branch breaks and falls with a thud.

Moisture can also be a danger when temperatures plunge. Delicate, white hoar frost sprinkled on twigs and branches looks delightful, but again, appearances can be deceptive. This phenomenon also originates in fog, this time when the temperature drops below freezing point. It is dangerous not only to you but also to the trees. If these weather conditions persist for days, frost crystals accumulate until perfectly healthy branches break off or whole trees crack open under their weight. Where I live in Germany, these conditions happen every five to ten years.

There is another icy danger on trees that I have observed just once in my professional life: a coating of ice. A light drizzle persisted for three days when the temperature hovered just below freezing. A frozen transparent layer less than a half-inch (one centimeter) thick lay like a glaze over the whole forest. All the younger trees were bent over under its weight, some of them almost to the ground. The tips of the older conifers broke off and crashed down. Hikers stayed home because the forest paths were more like competitive luge runs than walking trails.

The icy coating happens when snow falls through a layer of warm air, which melts the snowflakes into raindrops. If these raindrops then travel quickly through a layer of cold air, they don't have time to freeze (if they did, they would turn into sleet), but the cold layer has brought their temperature so low that after these super-cooled drops have flowed around whatever surface they land on, they immediately turn to ice. Severe ice storms caused considerable damage to trees and power lines in the American South in 1994 and in New England and eastern Quebec in 1998.

For forest visitors, the danger of branches falling under the weight of snow, layers of hoar frost, or excess humidity is not that high—no higher than the chances of being struck by lightning—so, I wouldn't give a second thought to going out hiking in foggy or snowy conditions. If there's a thunderstorm, ice storm, or high winds, however, you should stay at home, because then whole trees could break and fall.

~ 17 ~

Relying on the Forest to Survive

WE ALL NEED access to clean water to live. Once, years ago, when I was walking in England's Lake District, I would have given anything for clean water. At the small bed and breakfast where we were staying, each member of the family was given a lovingly prepared bag lunch. We stashed them away in our day packs. The surprise came when we took our first break high up on a hillside.

There was plenty to eat, but just one small box of apple juice per person. The fault was mine, because I ought to have checked the bags at breakfast to see what was inside. We soon drained the drink boxes, and then we had a long hike, all the while getting thirstier and thirstier. Not that there weren't enough burbling streams around. We passed one every fifteen minutes. However, up in the hills, we were walking with and surrounded by thousands of sheep that, unfortunately, were defecating into the streams. What a shame that was. We threw ourselves upon the first café we found when we reached a valley and immediately ordered copious quantities of water and lemonade. So, no matter how long or short your hike, it is always a good idea to bring an ample supply of drinking water. Even in the most remote places, whether sheep are about or not, it is not a good idea to drink water from springs or streams unless you have some means of sterilizing it. And cafés with lemonade are often in short supply.

If you're thinking of foraging for food, think again. It's actually quite difficult to find food in the forest. Little wonder that in hunter-gatherer times, the heavily forested area now called Germany could sustain a population of no more than ten thousand people. For large mammals (and that's what we are) forests are not fully stocked supermarkets just waiting for customers. You have to travel a long way to find food. That's why large predators have territories that cover many square miles. If their hunting areas were any smaller, they wouldn't be able to find enough prey animals to eat. And what about us? Our forebears' forest territories were twenty-five hundred times larger than the areas we now squeeze into in cities. They roamed over four square miles (ten square kilometers) per person, whereas we are restricted, on average, to a "territory" of a mere forty thousand square feet or so (four thousand square meters). We live and work in these tiny spaces, which are also covered with the infrastructure that supports our modern way of life: streets, railroad tracks, government offices, shops, agricultural land, and forests. We cram two thousand people into an area that supported just one of our ancestors.

If you embark on your own personal small survival venture, you can experience just how far civilization has removed us from our roots and our original sensations of taste. At one time I organized survival training workshops

Gray squirrel, Ocala National Forest, Florida

in the forest I manage. I allowed the participants to bring only three items: a sleeping bag, a cup, and a knife. We walked to a remote part of the forest and camped out there for the weekend. Because the workshop usually took place between May and September, you'd expect to find enough to eat. Mushrooms, berries, nuts: what more do you need to stay full for forty-eight-hours? Well, you can put aside thoughts about this delightful culinary trio. First, these items are only available for a few weeks and second, except for nuts, they are not a particularly good source of calories. And the nuts, as I know from long personal experience, are usually all gathered up by the squirrels before they have time to ripen.

Other fruits of the forest are there for the picking, although perhaps not in quite the same abundance.

Depending on where you live you might find blackberries, salmonberries, huckleberries, blueberries, or even tart wild apples—which brings up another issue. If you pick them, are you depriving the forest animals of food? Bears, deer, birds, snails, and insects depend on them and have difficulty finding alternate sources for the calories they need. So, take some to taste but remember the animals out there have no other options.

There's another reason you shouldn't eat too many berries. Although popping sweet blackberries and tiny, aromatic wild strawberries into your mouth all day long sounds idyllic, I'd like to interject a word of caution. I experienced a day exactly like this on one of the survival trips I was leading. It was a hot day in July. The whole group wandered through a clearing overgrown with blackberries. Large, black, sun-ripened fruit gleamed on the bushes. Hurray! We dropped everything and spent two hours filling our stomachs. However, two hours later, the stomachs of most participants were empty once again. The huge quantity of acid from the fruit had overwhelmed their digestive systems and quite a few of them found themselves throwing up the berries they had consumed.

As for nuts, roasted beechnuts (never eat them raw) are a delicacy. As the nuts are 50 percent oil, they will tide you over for a while, but you find them only every three to five years. Acorns are basically poisonous. However, if you peel them, boil them repeatedly, and change the water each time to get rid of the tannic acids, you can eat them, and they are packed with calories. Dried and ground up, they can be used in place of flour. However, as oaks also bear fruit only every three to five years, you will have trouble finding enough of them. Hickory nuts are an option in the South but be very sure you are not snacking on poisonous buckeye nuts as the two look very similar. Mushrooms, another fall staple, aren't much good because they are mostly water and contain hardly any calories at all. Or to be more accurate, we have great difficulty breaking them down and we excrete the half-digested remains. There is also the issue of which are edible and which will kill you if you eat them. Never taste a mushroom if you don't know precisely what it is.

If you can find berries, nuts, and mushrooms only in the fall, what can you find earlier in the year? One source of food that is particularly abundant is the cambium of spruce trees. The cambium is the growth layer of a tree, and it lies directly under the bark. The inner side of this layer grows wood, the outer side grows bark. In winter, the tree doesn't contain much water and it's almost impossible to separate the bark from the trunk. From March on, however, as soon as the spruce wakes from its winter sleep and starts to pump water up out of the ground again, it's easy to take a knife and peel the outer skin off the tree. This works particularly well in May, when the bark comes off in long strips.

So as not to damage a standing tree, it's best to experiment with a spruce downed by one of the previous winter's storms. Once you've removed the bark, the gleaming inner wood will be revealed. Now, where might you find the cambium? It's right there shining at you, because it's very moist. Take the flat side of your knife blade and scrape it along the wood to peel off milky strips. Voilà! The strips taste a bit like a woody carrot that has lost its sweetness. In addition to vitamins, they contain sugar and other carbohydrates. Pound for pound, cambium is one of the most nutritious foods in the forest and also one of the tastiest. And that's why those deer, bears, and porcupines we discussed in a previous chapter are so keen on peeling off bark to get at it. (Bears, by the way, often snack on skunk cabbage to get their digestive systems going again after their winter sleep before they move on to devouring cambium and whatever else they can find in the forest.)

A woody carrot as a culinary delight? Yes, indeed it is, and if a woody carrot doesn't sound delicious, we have only ourselves to blame. Real food straight from nature usually tastes bitter or sour. It's also often tough and fibrous and can be found only in small amounts, which means you have to spend the whole day searching for it. That makes cambium a special treat. The fact that we no longer know how to treasure it has to do with the evolution of food. In the past few decades, food has been shaped by ruthless competition. Our taste buds have been the judges, and what they crave are calories and novelty—our genetic inheritance from times long past.

We instinctively crave fat, sugar, salt, or concentrated carbohydrates. Ten thousand years ago that made sense. After all, back then there were hardly any calorie-stuffed foods, and if people were lucky enough to find any, they needed to eat them right away. Now we have modern supermarkets with their shelves full to overflowing, we don't have to do that anymore, but we can't just turn off our instinctive programming. Instead, foodstuffs are continually being optimized until they match our subconscious desires as exactly as possible.

Only products tailored to our inherited cravings survive in the marketplace, and then only until something even tastier pops up. The result? Broadly speaking, everything tastes roughly the same. Perhaps you think I'm exaggerating, but the proof is out there, growing in the forest. Try eating fresh ripe berries from salal or mountain ash, or a salad made from miner's lettuce and dandelions. Even thinking about those menu choices makes my mouth pucker; after all, in this respect, I am just as damaged by civilization as the next person. And viewed from this perspective, cambium is a real gift, at least between March and July. After that, the trees are preparing for winter once again and begin to dry out on the inside. Now you have to chip the bark off in small pieces to get to the cambium that lies hidden underneath.

Other spring options are tender leafy greens. You can harvest the tips of stinging nettles when they are young. Cooking removes their sting. Many people like to sauté them lightly in a pan or steam them like spinach. Ramps, also known as wild leeks, are one of the first spring greens to emerge at higher elevations from Georgia to Canada. To harvest them sustainably, use a sharp knife to cut a single leaf and leave the rest of the leaves and the roots so the plant can grow another year. Fiddleheads, the early growth of the ostrich fern, are another early spring delicacy. Be careful, though, because not all ferns that produce fiddleheads are edible, and some are toxic. It's best to cook fiddleheads before you eat them.

Some plants offer sustenance for more than one season because you can eat the stems. If you're foraging in damp places, for example, cattails are an option. Then there is invasive Japanese knotweed. It tastes a bit like lemony rhubarb although, like rhubarb, only certain parts of it are safe to eat and then only at certain times of the year. The good thing about eating Japanese knotweed is that you know you are doing the forest a favor by getting rid of it.

The roots of wild plants such as dandelions are an option. You need to thoroughly wash these pale, thin sources of nourishment, although even then you'll notice the grit when you bite into them. If you cut the roots into small pieces, roast them carefully, and grind them into a powder in the frying pan using a mug, you can brew a sort of root coffee. It's brown and the taste is bittersweet and vaguely reminiscent of home—if you've been away long enough.

If foraging in the forest interests you, I suggest investing in a comprehensive book for your area so you can read up on which poisonous plants (or plant parts) you need to stay away from, what is tasty (rather than just edible), how to harvest sustainably, and how best to prepare what you pick.

If you're willing to expand your repertoire beyond plants, you can try other delicacies out there in the forest. Beetle larvae, for instance. Where I live, the longhorn beetle is a good candidate. The larvae are about an inch (a couple of centimeters) or slightly longer, and they're flat and white with a dark brown head. They're flat because they search for the last crumbs of food under the bark of dead trees. While they're at it, they shred the bark with their large pincers, turning the dried-out cambium into dust. These larvae are packed full of protein and if you must fend for yourself in the forest, you might have no choice but to pop them into your mouth. But don't be too hasty because this snack bites back. I advise you to eat the head to start, and then enjoy the rest. The taste is nutty and earthy and if you can shut off the images running through your head, beetle larvae rank right up there with cambium. Big chunks of trunks left to rot after the last timber harvest are usually good places to find them. Choose a piece of wood and turn it over so the bark lying on the damp ground is on top. Now you can start removing sections of rotting bark with your pocketknife to reveal the pale creatures living underneath.

If you don't find beetle larvae, at least you will find sow bugs or the closely related pill bugs, also known as roly polies. You should now banish from your mind any associations that might interfere with your enjoyment of your snack: the underside of the doormat at your house, for instance, or dark spaces such as vents to the cellar. The reason pill bugs seek out these dark, moist spaces is that they are terrestrial crustaceans. Instead of lungs, they have gills modified to work on land, but their breathing apparatus works only when they are damp.

If you eat them raw, you can tell immediately from the taste that pill bugs are related to shrimp. In order to make the culinary event less of a shock for both the ingredients and your taste buds, however, I suggest you sauté your finds in a pan with a little oil. I always bring both along on my survival tours to ease the transition from civilization to wilderness. And indeed, after just a few seconds, the sautéed bugs taste like potato chips. Lightly salted, the only thing that betrays their provenance is their appearance.

Anthills are also a great place to find food. The little creatures crawl around by the tens of thousands. Just reach out and grab a handful. You can turn your live victims into dead ones by giving them a quick squeeze. That way they can no longer bite your tongue. But, as I mentioned earlier, pay attention when you squat down next to an anthill. In no time at all, you'll find ants crawling into your shoes and up your pant legs, inside as well as out.

I've often heard people say, "I won't eat that, but I could if I had to." I think just the opposite is true. When I led my tours, the participants were always ready to try just about anything the first afternoon. Their stomachs were still full of meals they had eaten at home or at a restaurant on the journey down. And every discovery of larvae was an amusing test of their adventurous spirit. The second day, however, when their stomachs had been growling for quite some time and fatigue had set in as a result of all the physical activity, the joy in experimenting was long gone. Larvae? No thank you, we can wait. Tomorrow, we'll be home. People preferred a quick lie down on a mattress of brushwood, where they attempted to nap so they could forget the grumbling in their stomachs.

And what about more traditional fare? Maybe you could try your hand at hunting? Apart from the fact that you'd need a hunting license and a regional permit for the area where you're staying, the chances of finding enough game for you to survive are slim. It could be days before a likely target walks by the spotting scope on your rifle and by that time you will have weakened considerably. And as a rule, who carries a gun around so they can get food in case of an emergency? It's much easier and more productive to set your sights on tiny critters or the earthworms I mentioned earlier in this book.

You might have more success with a fishing rod or small net, but again that really depends on the abundance of life in the streams you pass and whether you packed your fishing gear. And, of course, local regulations about whether you can keep and eat any fish you manage to catch. Bears are adept at scooping salmon out of rivers with their paws, but you are less likely to succeed with just your bare hands. One of the aquatic creatures you can catch by hand, however, is crayfish. Crayfish hide under rocks in shallow streams and lakes in southern forests. You can wade in carefully and turn over flat rocks to try to find them. If you do reach for one, be careful it doesn't grab you with its pincers and, again, know the regulations regarding their harvest.

You can have fun tasting wild food, but plants and mushrooms are unlikely to sustain you for long, some are poisonous, and regulations cover harvesting food from the wild, be it animal or vegetable. It's best to snack lightly only on those foods you can positively identify and to bring provisions from home, so you don't go hungry if your day takes a seriously unexpected turn.

~ 18 ~

Comfort in
the Forest

SOMETIMES IT GETS COLD, even in summer, mostly when night falls on the forest. It's nice to have a fire at these times because feeling cold is just as bad as feeling hungry. If you are on public land, the first thing to be aware of are the local rules. Many areas want you to burn only locally sourced wood and have rules about whether it's okay to collect dead-wood for your fire. Depending on the weather conditions, open fires may be banned completely. Insects and diseases can hitchhike to new areas in firewood and the majority of forest fires are started by people, so do your part not to contribute to these problems. Most parks post the fire danger on any given day and the rules will be available at the park entrance or visitors center.

When you read how easily wildfires start, it seems that starting a campfire shouldn't be difficult. Not even close. It's usually quite tricky, especially in wet weather. The cold drops of rain soak through everything, often accompanied by a light breeze that immediately extinguishes the flame on whatever you are using to light the fire. If you like, you can make your own tinderbox to carry in your pack for just such an occasion. The setup is somewhat complex, but it makes it much easier to get the spark you need to start a campfire in the forest.

First you need a metal tin of the kind used for old-fashioned candies such as mints or fruit drops. Poke a hole in the lid with a nail. Fill the tin with scraps of cotton from worn-out underwear or linens and put the lid on. The next time you barbeque, place the tin near the glowing coals and wait. You'll see a small, white plume of steam that will then disappear. Now you can set the closed tin to one side to cool. When you open it, you will find carbonized cloth inside—all done.

Next, you will need a piece of flint, the kind of hard, angular rock you can find on many beaches or in some streams. And, finally, a piece of carbon (not stainless) steel, ideally bent into a D-shape so you can hold the straight side of the "D" in your palm with the curved side around the outside of your fist. You can find such things on the internet or at flea markets. All you are missing is a bit of hemp fiber of the kind used as a thread sealant for plumbing pipes (you can buy it in hardware stores). Now your equipment will look like a fire starter from olden times because this is how people used to do it.

To create a spark, take the steel in one hand (with the curve outside your fingers) and a piece of flint in the other. Using your thumb, clamp a piece of the carbonized cloth (known as charcloth) over the flint. Now strike a glancing blow to one of the sharp edges of the stone and you'll get a spark. The goal is to knock a spark onto the cloth so the ember spreads through the cloth. Now put the glowing cloth into a ball of separated hemp fibers and blow gently and constantly until the ember grows and eventually the ball bursts into flame.

Quickly pile thin twigs over the burning hemp (not too many and not all at once or you will extinguish the flame), and there you are, you've lit your campfire. If it's later in the season and wildflowers and rushes are producing fluffy seed heads, these can be added with the twigs to get the fire going. Birch bark, pinecones, and the dry underside of moss are all readily combustible. With a little bit of practice, you'll find you can reliably light a fire the old-fashioned way. And, of course, you don't have to save your tinderbox for emergencies. It's fun to use it to light a fire to toast bread or grill hot dogs along the trail. If you're hiking with kids, sparking flames this way is always a highlight.

Once you've got your spark to catch, what burns well? Birch bark makes a great base because of the oils it contains. Start by taking a knife and scraping the outside surface of the bark to produce a small pile of fine shavings. Make sure you're in a sheltered spot when you do this, so the shavings don't blow away. Next, peel thin strips off the outside of the bark. It's easier to do this if you bend the bark a bit. Now you have shavings, thin strips, and leftover pieces of bark. Start by igniting the shavings with the spark, gradually add the thin strips, and then add the larger pieces of bark once the fire has taken. (Or, if you're like Jane, who did not make a tinderbox to take with her, start your campfire with fire starter and a match and then add a section of birch bark just to watch how long and hot it burns.) Birch bark is so flexible that you can also weave kindling from it if you have some time on your hands. Rip the bark into narrow strips. Then weave the strips together in a pattern of your choice.

Resinous wood from dead conifers is also great to get a fire going because it burns even when it is wet. First you need to find a downed pine or spruce and look for branch stubs. The tree will have pumped resin into the branch stubs while it was still alive to keep insects and infection from entering its trunk through the rotting wood of dead branches. The ends of the branches will have rotted off, but the stubs full of resin will still be intact. Saw off a few branch stubs. They will have a pinkish interior and will smell distinctively piney. Split the stubs into three- to four-inch (seven- to ten-centimeter) chunks with a knife or a small pickax. Take one of the chunks and, using a knife, shave little curls on the lower part to increase its surface area. Create a spark to light the curls and use that chunk to start your fire, carefully piling on the other chunks of fatwood (as it is called) until you have a good starter fire going. If you happen to have a metal pencil sharpener with you, you can break off a few pencil-sized slivers of wood, sharpen them, and add the shavings to encourage the fire.

In wet weather, you'll quickly become aware of a problem: where are you going to find dry wood to feed the fire? The rain has soaked through all the woody debris on the ground. Even the largest ball of burning hemp will smolder only briefly before going out and strips of birch bark burn well but not for long. A solution to this problem is growing in the trees, especially evergreen conifers such as spruce or pines. Thanks to the umbrella-like arrangement of their branches, the ground around their trunks is mostly dry, and here you will find ample quantities of thin, dead twigs. If local rules allow, you can gather these up for your fire. They will burn even after days of bad weather, and once you have lit a fire with their help, you can add the wetter branches.

If you have permission to light a fire somewhere other than in the firepits the park has provided, place it only on ground that you have cleared of debris. Rake away all the

Branch stub, Deep River, Ontario

needles, leaves, and humus, and then, ideally, put a circle of stones around the area. You clear the area because, even though rain has often soaked through the upper layer making it safe to light a fire there, deeper down there can still be debris that is bone-dry. Especially under moss, you often find plant material that could easily catch on fire. Once on a rainy day in winter, I had to drive out to the forest I manage to extinguish the smoldering remains of a fire a hiker had left behind after a rest stop. I had brought along a five-gallon (twenty-liter) container of water for the purpose, but it soon became clear that wasn't going to be enough. Although the burning area was less than a couple of feet wide (no more than half a meter), the fire kept smoldering under the damp layer of moss. The moss, acting as an impermeable roof, shed the water I was pouring on the fire to extinguish it. I couldn't put the fire out until I had completely removed the and a layer of thick, corky bark that insulates the trunk. The dense array of long needles on the seedling's growing tip retains moisture, while the silvery scales covering the tip reflect the heat. Once the seedling has stored enough energy in its taproot, it shoots up. It doesn't put energy into growing branches until its growing tip is six feet (two meters) off the ground, which is higher than the level of a ground fire. When a longleaf pine matures, its scaly bark flakes off in a fire to carry the heat away from the inner part of the tree.

A mature longleaf pine savannah with its widely spaced trees and understory of wire grass actively invites frequent fires. The needles and twigs it drops are full of resin and highly flammable, as are the dry stalks of the grass that grows below. When fires are frequent, there is not much forest debris for them to burn and as the longleaf pines do not grow branches into the fire zone, the flames stay low to the ground. These savannah ground fires regenerate rather than destroy. Fires become fatal for trees when there is enough fuel for them to climb up into the crowns. That is when they rage hot and burn down large portions of the forest.

Ponderosa pines in the West also grow in dry areas where lightning strikes are frequent, and they have many of the same adaptations as longleaf pines: thick, insulating bark, long needles that retain moisture, and deep root systems. Old-growth ponderosa pines often grow in patchy groups of differently aged trees. The trees within these groups, like the longleaf pines in the savannah systems, are often widely spaced. The open spaces make it more difficult for a flammable understory to build up and for fire to spread from tree to tree. You may well encounter prescribed burns and forest thinning operations in parks in the South. The park rangers are re-creating the conditions produced by the naturally occurring ground fires that are now extinguished the moment they begin to burn because human structures are encroaching ever farther into the forest.

And then there are the coniferous forests of the Pacific Northwest where natural fires hardly ever happen because the climate is so damp. The trees grow huge and a lot of debris builds up on the forest floor. When these forests burn, which they do every century or so, they burn fiercely. Trees are killed, but the fire rarely consumes them completely. Eventually, the fire-damaged trees fall, rot, and contribute to the slow but sure regeneration of the forest.

Now, where were we with your campfire? Everything has gone according to plan. You have found enough food to eat and managed to build and extinguish your fire. You are pleasantly full. Internal processes are going into overdrive and at some point, the food you have taken in at one end needs to come out at the other. But who wants to attend to big business when there's no toilet paper around? Because you don't normally snack on forest fare, there are a few additional problems as your stool—we might as well come right out and say it—will be unusually runny. But, here too, Nature comes to your aid with the soft cushions of moss that grow on old tree stumps. You can peel them off in sheets and, as they have about the same tensile strength as toilet paper, you can use them in the same way you would the paper off a roll in the bathroom. If there's been a shower that morning or it's early in the day and dew is still on the ground, the moisture will transform this plant material into a handy wet wipe.

Having found some moss, you need to choose with care the secluded spot where you intend to do your business. And I don't mean simply avoiding the cameras that hunters or park rangers put up to spot animals passing by. I am referring to the pesky little creatures you need to be aware of. Once your pants are down and you're in a state of relative helplessness, little midges and gnats will particularly enjoy attacking your exposed skin. This happens most often when the part of the forest you find yourself in is low lying and slightly soggy with the trees far enough apart to let some sunshine through. A better choice would be a shaded spot, preferably at the crest of a hill or, if that's not possible, at least on the upper slopes. A brisk breeze is ideal because small flying insects will get blown away. If bags for human waste have not been provided at the trailhead, as they often are nowadays for hikes in remote areas, as a friendly gesture to other hikers, I suggest you bury the remains.

Your digestive system has been filled, then emptied, and those basic processes have taken the whole day, because you've only been able to find small handfuls of food here and there, and it's taken hours for you to find enough to still your hunger. Before the day finally draws to a close, you still need to deal with the issue of a good night's sleep. If you've decided to trust yourself completely to the forest and have left your tent and sleeping bag behind, what you need to do now is scout around for recently downed conifer branches with green needles on them. You'll use these to build your bed. Lie the greenery on the ground so the curve to the branches points up. The branches will have some give to them like the latticework on a bed frame. Position the thick central ribs of the branches to the left and right so they form the edges of the bed and the softer side branches overlap in the middle. The higher you stack the branches, the more comfortable you will be.

And it pays to be careful. Participants on my weekend survival camps in the woods have often built uncomfortable beds by stacking the branches any which way, despite my instructions. Their lack of attention comes back to haunt them in the night when bits of wood poke them in the back, so they get as little sleep as the princess lying on the pea. If you lay everything down as you should, you create a sort of basin that will cradle you securely during the night. That's important, because the bed always ends up being at a slight angle, which means that you slowly but surely get closer to the edge each time you turn over and will find yourself on the hard ground come morning. Raised edges keep you centered and free to dream in peace. Although sometimes you might have difficulty falling asleep right away because of the unfamiliar noises around you. I don't mean the odd hoot, most of which stops by midnight. I mean the rustling of beetles and other insects in the branches above you and, unfortunately, beneath you, as well. All this activity means you need to be very tired before you can finally fall sleep.

You wake up, perhaps after a rather unsettled night, and wonder what time it is. Well, do you mean the time on your watch or phone, or forest time? The two are not quite the same thing. I have a reputation for being a bit of a time freak: if I don't wear a watch on my wrist I feel as though I'm not properly dressed. It's not just that I have a lot of appointments to keep (I might be a forester by profession, but this job is not as laid back as you might think), but also that I love the ticking of mechanical clocks. It doesn't matter if they are grandfather clocks or clocks designed to sit on a shelf, their muffled chimes remind me of times past.

Whether we rely on such hand-crafted rarities or on the digital displays on our cell phones, we've all internalized to some extent the divisions of the day. But your timepiece and the forest clock don't always agree. The first disconnect is astronomical. Thanks to the differences in longitude between one place and the next, the time on your watch or phone doesn't correspond exactly with the position of the sun. For instance, the discrepancy for Hümmel, the village where I live, is about half an hour from Middle European Time (MEZ), which corresponds to sunrise on the fifteenth easterly line of longitude. If you are anywhere along this line, the sun at noon will be directly south of you. The farther off this line you are, the further off the time on your watch will be. For instance, when your watch registers the time as noon, the actual time in Hümmel according to the position of the sun would be just 11:30 a.m. The village is way to the western side of Germany, and therefore the Earth has to turn for another thirty minutes before the sun hits its zenith here.

The difference is even more pronounced when we take daylight savings time into account, which brings us to our second error. We turn the clocks forward by an hour, increasing the deviation by sixty minutes. Then if I look up at the sky above Hümmel at noon, the sun is in the 10:30 a.m. position. Why am I talking about this? Because the forest knows nothing of human timekeeping and the rhythms under the trees follow the true position of the sun. The forest, just as we do, recognizes the difference between day and night, dawn and dusk, and all the gradations in between. It's just that humans and forests have different methods of keeping time—and they're not always in sync.

Birds are amazing timekeepers and in the forest you might do better to trust them than your watch. If you listen to the dawn chorus, you can hear how sensitive birds are to increasing amounts of light as the sun rises. So that each singer has some time to be heard, each species has its own time slot, or perhaps more accurately its own position on the sun dial, when it is center stage. While skylarks in Germany start singing one-and-a-half hours before sunrise, the chiffchaff doesn't get in the mood for music until sixty minutes later. If you can identify the species that live close to you, you will be able to put together your own personal bird clock by listening to their song. One thing all songbirds have in common is this: as soon as the sun comes up over the horizon, they start serenading the world. I should mention that a natural clock such as this is useful only for people who get up early and only for the six months of summer.

You've checked the time and unfortunately you need to get back home. As you're packing up camp, remember to take everything you brought in with you. I'm often asked if there's such a thing as "good" trash. That is to say, are there things we can leave behind in the forest and not worry about the impact they will have? This question comes up a lot for hikers. Who wants to put a mushy banana peel or a soggy apple core in their backpack? Or the well-used tissue that's already beginning to fall apart? A vigorous toss will consign these items to the underbrush. After all, this is organic material. In a few months, it will decompose and become humus. However, I would advise against throwing even compostable material away for several reasons. For starters, fruit is often coated with a spray or wax to make it attractively shiny. These coatings slow the rate of decomposition and leave chemical compounds in the soil that don't belong there. The same can be said of the tissue. And there's something else I should mention in connection with tissues. Because they are white, they stand out and broadcast to everyone passing by that there is trash here. Trash attracts more trash, which is why most forest shelters no longer have waste bins. Once these bins are full, people

~ 19 ~

Striking Out Cross-Country

WE'VE TALKED ABOUT staying on trails on public land for your own comfort and safety, but sometimes circumstances crop up when you need to make a detour or perhaps you get lost and really need to get home before dark. This happened to Jane once when she first moved to North America from Europe and hadn't quite adapted to the large scale of the landscape. She and her hiking partner set off into the forest in northern Saskatchewan armed with a map and compass. They were fine on the compass direction, but not so good at calculating distance. Everything is so much bigger in North America than in Europe.

After a while, they were lost, and it was getting time to leave the forest before dark. They knew that if they headed east, they would eventually encounter a road, and so off they went. Past the stream with bear tracks along the banks. Past the moose skeleton. (If the moose hadn't made it out, what chance did they have?) All the while being eaten alive by mosquitoes, which meant that Jane kept her rain jacket on all the time despite the heat. Eventually, they made it to the road, sweaty and covered with twigs and leaves. And so,

I would like to tell you about some of the tips I have learned to make bushwhacking more pleasant should you ever find yourself in a position when you need (or choose) to set off cross-country.

In forests of spruce, pine, and Douglas fir, especially if they are planted, the trees may be growing so close together that their dead lower branches block your way. It's as though the trees were locking arms on purpose to keep you out. I sometimes resort to walking backward so I can force my way through. That way, branches don't hit me in the face or, worse yet, poke me in the eye. Deciduous forests are far more welcoming, although if there's grass growing under the trees, you should avoid walking through it. Morning dew or raindrops clinging to the blades will soak through your boots in an instant. Even built-in waterproof membranes won't keep out the damp indefinitely in such terrain.

Do you know the old rule about how to find your way by looking for moss? In the Northern Hemisphere, it is said to grow on the north side of trees, because moss thrives in moist conditions and therefore loves shade. However, if you rely on this rule in the forest, I guarantee you will get lost. The reason for this is that although moss likes shade, it is the moisture it finds there, rather than the shade itself, that dictates where moss will grow.

Trees rarely grow ramrod straight. Most trunks develop a slight banana-shaped bend. Deciduous trees gather water with their branches and direct it down their trunks to their roots. The bend influences the water's route. A small stream of water flows on the upper side of the bend, but on the lower side, water droplets fall off so the bark below the bend doesn't retain any of the moisture. This means moss doesn't grow there, but forms a thick cushion on the wet upper side.

All that does is show where the bend is. It doesn't give any indication of the compass direction. And because every tree bends a little differently, the moss appears randomly here and there. Test this for yourself the next time you go out for a hike. You will notice, incidentally, that moss rarely grows on conifers because their branches direct rain away from their trunks and so they, at least, won't add to your confusion. And, of course, if you are hiking out in western Oregon, where everything is coated in moss, you will need to keep moving to make sure the moss doesn't start growing on you while you are out on the trail!

Sometimes you know the direction you should be going, but there are obstacles in your way. If you're hiking in an area where blackberries run amok, they can be a challenge. I don't mean the berries, of course, though they might slow you down if you stop to pick some. Most of the year, all you'll find are tangled thorny canes arching up to form impenetrable barriers often ten feet (three meters) tall or more. If for some reason you need to cross an area overgrown with these bushes, try walking like a stork. Well, in Germany I would walk like a stork but seeing as you don't have many storks in North America, except in the South, a heron might offer a better image to hold in your mind. Tread carefully with one foot on the uppermost cane, then put your weight down on it and take your next step onto the next-lowest cane. You'll look ridiculous, but usually no one will see you. If you're impatient or don't want to take such awkward steps, you can quickly get caught up in the canes. They'll then tighten their grip around your legs like a lasso until it's almost impossible to free yourself from their unwanted embrace. Often when you take your next step, you end up falling into the tangle of thorns—ouch!

There's also a danger of falling when you walk down a steep slope. Not because you can't keep your balance, although that might be a problem, but because disaster lurks under leaf litter or snow in the form of dead branches where the bark has rotted away, exposing the smooth wood underneath. These branches are usually oriented in the direction of the slope, which is to say pointing straight downhill. If you step on one, as you put your weight down, you will slide downhill as though you'd stepped on a patch of ice. As I mentioned earlier in the book, this has happened to me even though I should know better. By the time I realize what I've stepped on, it's usually too late to save myself. I lose my balance, flail my arms, and then crash down onto the ground.

To be on the safe side, avoid steep slopes, especially in wet weather. The trails made by wild game are a good option if you need to navigate a slope. Animals have the same problems you do, and therefore they stick to well-used paths with even, packed-down surfaces. The trails might be narrow, usually no more than a dozen inches or so (about thirty centimeters) wide, but that's all you need for a good footing. On long descents, a number of these game paths are often evenly distributed across the slope, running parallel to one another. So, you can make your way downhill by dropping down from one path to the next, following in the tracks the animals have left.

Once you arrive at the bottom of the valley, you might well find you need to cross a stream. Up until now you've managed to keep your boots dry and there's no need to get them wet now. Most hikers traveling off the beaten path will attempt to jump from one side of the stream to the other. That should be relatively easy. After all, the banks of most streams are no more than a generous stride apart. Everyone should be able to jump that far. And that's true, assuming the land on either side of the stream is dry. Streams with relatively flat banks, however, can lure you into a false sense of security. Flat banks tend to get saturated from below, which creates a small marshy area on either side. If you take a flying leap, you might well find yourself landing in mud with cold water oozing up and into your boots. How can you avoid that happening to you?

The first thing to do is to find a spot where the stream bank is steeper. There's a good chance the banks here are reinforced by rocks under the soil. You also improve the odds of getting to the other side with dry feet and clean shoes if you cross close to tree roots, which form a protective liner under the streambed. If the stream is too wide for you to bound across in a single leap, check the streambed and the water level.

It's easiest to cross in a place where the stream is no deeper than the sides of your shoes are high, and where you can see rocks in the water. Then you can wade in with confidence. If the rocks are small, they will have been washed clean of mud over time and will usually be as solid and stable as a city sidewalk. Well, perhaps not quite as stable as they can be a bit slippery, so put your feet down slowly and firmly before you trust your full weight to them. This is especially important in fast-flowing streams with larger rocks, where the force of the water may have piled them up on top of each other. In that case, test each one carefully with one foot or a hiking pole before putting your full weight on it, just in case it wobbles when you step on it.

In all my time hiking through the woodland I manage, I have never sunk into a streambed, but I have often sunk into saturated banks. The one small danger when wading through a stream is that you might misjudge the depth. But in that case even though you will get wet, you won't get dirty!

Just one more word of caution about streams. If you're hiking through forests up in the mountains, the streams you come across may well be fed by snowfields or glaciers. A stream that is bubbling merrily in the morning can become a raging torrent by afternoon after many hours of snowmelt. So be careful how you time your hike. You don't want to find yourself stuck on the wrong side of the stream as the sun goes down.

Sometimes what you encounter at the bottom of a slope is not a sparkling stream but a muddy swampy bottomland that stretches in all directions. Despite the excellent construction of your hiking boots, mud soup will spill over the tops if you sink in too deep. So, it's not a bad idea to reduce the impact of your boot (and therefore how far it will sink into the mud) by increasing the size of the area you step on. You could do this, for example, by finding branches to use as stepping stones. When you step on them, you distribute your weight over a wider area. You just need to check the wood isn't rotten, or it will break with a sharp crack and you'll find yourself sinking even deeper into the mud.

Branches are not always lying around when you need them. If you can't find any, maybe you can use clumps of grass instead. Each little cushion sticks up out of the surrounding marsh like a small island, and they are surprisingly stable. If you make your way from clump to clump, you'll be able to get to the other side with dry feet. That works around streams, but, unfortunately—as Jane has discovered to her cost—not for marshland. In those areas, the grass clumps grow on muddy peat moss and become more and more unstable the farther into the marsh you go.

In wet weather, depending on the terrain, you may find mud building up on your boots, but luckily, this is the time when streams and ditches fill with water. Find a flat spot and step in to let the water wash away the mud. If you do this for no longer than a minute or two, your feet will stay dry even if you're wearing leather boots without a water-proof membrane. If there's no moving water handy, clumps of damp grass provide another option. Just drag your feet through them a few times (don't forget to drag your feet backward to get rid of mud on the heel). Your boots won't look perfect, but they won't drop large clods of dirt either. And what if there aren't any clumps of grass either? Then a vigorous scuffle through the underbrush can help. The small branches and twigs lying around on the ground act like brushes. If they don't do a good enough job, you can wipe away the last of the mud with a piece of moss. If it's been raining, the little green cushions will be soaked with fresh, clean rainwater, and you can use the moss as a wet wipe to clean your hands, as well. There, good as new.

~ 20 ~

Choosing Your Wardrobe

THE OUTDOOR CLOTHING business is booming. When you look at the catalogs, it's difficult to decide which pants, shoes, or jackets to buy. Even I would be at a loss if not for the reviews, and going to a store to try things on doesn't help much, either. A few ground rules will keep you from getting completely confused. The simplest one is to look at what the professionals are wearing. People who spend a lot of time outside don't cut corners when it comes to clothing.

Have you ever wondered why foresters always wear green? Hundreds of years ago, the answer might have been because of poachers. Even today there's the occasional plaque in some isolated spot in a German forest marking the place where one of my predecessors lost a heroic battle to someone who was up to no good. When dealing with the poachers of the past, effective camouflage could be a lifesaver.

Today, it's often the other way around. In areas where trees are being cut down, people wearing camouflage risk finding themselves crushed. Tree fellers work in groups and if they can't see their coworkers, they could topple trees in the wrong direction. Therefore, all workers should at the very least have some high-visibility orange patches on their safety clothing. Foresters, however, tend to walk alone through stands of trees deciding which should be taken down. They mark the trunks with spray paint or colored tape. In thick stands of trees, there's often no way to avoid bodily contact. To anyone who happens by as the forester is putting tape around a tree, it looks like they're giving the tree a big hug. Their clothes get smeared with traces of green algae, which are barely noticeable if they're wearing olive green in the first place.

If you're a hunter, the situation is different once again. To deer and feral hogs, it doesn't matter what color you wear. If you think green works particularly well as camouflage so you can spot game more easily, you're sorely mistaken. You still have the bulky outline of a large animal. It's much more important to break up your silhouette so the irregular pattern on your clothes blends in with the play of light and shadow in the underbrush. Think of a tiger, which melts into the background thanks to its vertical stripes. Hunters find themselves in an awkward position. On the one hand, to meet legal requirements they need to be highly visible, which means wearing orange. On the other, they want to see and shoot as much wild game as possible.

The clothing industry has stepped up and offers camouflage jackets sporting high-visibility colors. Does that sound contradictory? Maybe, but it works very well. My former boss in the forest service wore just such a jacket during a drive hunt and was almost run over by a roebuck: only at the last second did the deer realize my colleague wasn't a bush. The animal blundered because large forest mammals are partially color blind and can't tell red from green or yellow. To the eye of a wild animal, a jacket with a camouflage pattern blends into the background. The only exception is blue. Strictly speaking, deer and feral hogs, like most mammals, see only blue or not-blue, which means for your next "observation jacket," you have a wide range of colors to choose from.

Consider not only color but also material. Personally, I'm not a big fan of high-tech fabrics for jackets. Although the membranes reliably keep moisture out, they often break down after just a few years. I prefer clothes that serve me well for half a lifetime. A mix of cotton and synthetic fabric makes a good compromise, because this combination dries quickly but is still very hard wearing. Jackets and pants made from these materials will survive many trips through thorny underbrush relatively unscathed. And if the jacket, especially, is thick enough, you won't need a moisture-proof layer. It will take at least an hour for rain to make it through to your skin and usually that's enough time for you to find shelter, perhaps under a mighty old spruce.

In nasty weather sometimes even the best hiking boots don't keep your feet dry because the membrane, despite all assurances to the contrary, ends up letting water through. In this respect, boots are like jackets. The bonded fabric is particularly susceptible to breaking down where it creases, so after a while these boots let in just as much moisture as leather boots without any high-tech fabric. So, either you need to keep replacing your boots or you wear rubber boots when it rains. But which rubber boots should you choose? The cheaper ones are made of synthetic material and fail especially in winter, when they become rock hard. Their lack of pliability combined with frozen ground transforms them into something resembling ice skates. Apart from that, the cheap ones are not good for your feet, because they usually don't fit very well. It's easier to walk in rubber boots, which remain supple even in frosty weather and often have an inner sole designed for comfort. If you're going to go out in the cold, make sure there's plenty of room for a nice thick pair of woolen socks and maybe even toe warmers. Rubber boots are especially fun for kids so they can splash through puddles on the trails.

In cool or wet weather, layering is important. The goal is to keep warm without overheating. If you get so hot that you sweat, it will be almost impossible to dry your clothes out until you get home. What are your choices here? Wool stays warm when wet, but takes longer to dry than synthetics. Synthetics feel colder when wet, but dry more quickly than wool. Synthetics tend to smell more than wool, so you might want to take that into account depending on who your hiking companions are and what you plan to do after your hike. Pure cotton, common though it is for T-shirts, is the worst of both worlds: it loses all capacity to insulate when it gets wet and it takes a long time to dry.

To make sure you don't sweat when hiking, start with fewer clothes rather than more and then add them when you need them. If you're like Jane and really don't like to feel cold, this can require some self-control when you are standing around at the start of a hike before you've had a chance to warm up. Just grin and bear it for a while. You will generate heat as soon as you hit the trail. While you're hiking, remember you get warmer when hiking uphill and cool off as you expend less energy going downhill. Adjust your clothing accordingly. There's one local hike Jane does so often that she knows exactly when to unzip her jacket for the uphill climb and when to zip it back up again for the descent. Remember also to keep well hydrated, especially in winter when your body may not give many clues that you are losing moisture. A thermos of hot tea can make a winter hike feel more luxurious.

IN MANY AREAS, when you go out on a summer hike, one of the first questions that springs to mind is "Are there lots of ticks out there?" These little creatures have recently become a real concern, because they can lurk anywhere to sneakily attack us. I should be upfront about this. I cannot completely calm your fears. These tiny arachnids are indeed dangerous, although they can't help it.

I had my first run-in with these minuscule monsters when I was just starting out in my forest service job. I had been assigned to a training forest to spend a year gaining practical experience in the field. I was given a number of tasks, all of which required me to spend a lot of time walking around outside. On my first day, I arrived dressed in my favorite color: blue. In my mind, blue jeans and a blue jacket were appropriate attire for hands-on work in the forest. I immediately attracted sidelong glances: a would-be forester in blue? No one had ever seen such a thing. Crushed, the next Saturday I took myself to a shop that sold hunting apparel and purchased a pair of appropriately German knee-length pants, a shirt with imitation staghorn buttons, and an army jacket, all in olive green. The sidelong glances disappeared and yet, as I would soon learn, I was still wearing the wrong clothes. My mother had knit me long socks to match my knee-length britches and in the heat of the summer sun they were extremely itchy. But no matter, I felt like a real forester and I was in the best of moods as I strode out through the underbrush in a clear-cut. My good mood lasted until I got home and undressed to take a shower. Then I noticed little dots up my legs. Ticks! Immediately, I began pulling them off and counting how many were attached to my skin. Appalled, I stopped when I got to fifty and quickly removed the rest.

I know now that I made two rookie mistakes when I walked through the forest that day. First, my clothes. Ticks like to hang out in the lower layers of vegetation up to about knee height. And my clothes at this level consisted of knee-length knit socks with holes between the stitches that the little creatures could easily crawl through to get to my skin. My second error was the route I chose. Deer like to spend their days in grassy areas dotted with small bushes. Deer happen to be the main host for ticks, which means a particularly high concentration of these blood suckers wait in the deer's daytime hangouts for unsuspecting victims to pass by.

Here's what I learned from my experience. You can drastically reduce the danger of ending up with ticks on you if you dress and hike appropriately. Assuming you are hiking along a trail, you're unlikely to come across a tick. They cannot fall out of trees onto their victims. If that were the case, all it would take would be a breath of wind to blow the almost weightless arachnids quite some distance through the air. The transfer must happen via direct body contact when you brush past low-growing vegetation. But don't worry, the little pests are not lying in wait on every blade of grass or every bush: they could wait there forever. Although ticks can go a whole year without food, they likely don't enjoy that very much. Therefore, they prefer to hunt for victims along the edges of game trails, those narrow, beaten-down paths where deer and feral hogs regularly travel. This is where the engorged ticks fall to the ground after sating themselves with blood, this is where they lay their eggs, and this is where the juveniles later lurk. When the ground shakes and a certain scent wafts through the air, they know a large mammal is approaching. They get ready to embark on their life's journey. They extend their forelegs and climb aboard as soon as fur or skin is within their reach. Then they crawl to a spot where the skin is warm and thin enough for them to pierce with their mouthparts, and within twenty-four hours, they begin their meal of blood.

The tick takes its time finding a comfortable spot before settling down to feed, which gives you the opportunity to pick it off your skin or clothing and flick it back on the grass before it starts feeding. If you tuck your shirt into your pants and your pant legs into your socks, you make it more difficult for the ticks to get to your skin. Wear light-colored pants so roving ticks will stand out as black dots—dots because in the early stages of their life they are no bigger than a poppy seed and you have to look closely to see them. In my experience, you'll find 99 percent of the little creatures when you get back to a proper trail, check your legs below the knee, and pick off anything that looks suspicious.

If you overlook one of these little pests, it won't stay on your lower legs, but will start to move. Its goal is to find a moist, shaded spot—under a fold of skin, for example. One night I heard strange scratching sounds while I was in my sleeping bag. They weren't coming from the forest, but from inside my ear. A visit to the ear, nose, and throat doctor revealed that a tick had found its way to my eardrum and had begun sucking blood there. The procedure to remove it with a pair of tweezers was extremely painful, but at least it put an abrupt end to the unnerving scratching noise from its tiny legs. The moral of this story is that if you notice ticks on your legs after a hike, you should check the skin on every part of your body, just to be on the safe side. Clothing impregnated with tick repellent offers an added layer of protection.

And what should you do if one of these pesky little creatures ends up biting you despite the precautions you've taken? Remove it as soon as possible. Ticks are not like little screws, so don't try to remove them by turning them to the left or right, no matter what the internet says. The quickest thing is to take a pair of sharp-nosed (not flat-nosed) tweezers, grab them as close to the head as possible, and pull them up and out. It's important not to squeeze their bodies as you pull (which is why sharp-nosed tweezers are better than wide flat ones) or their bodily fluids will enter the small wound they have made and, unfortunately, these fluids can contain pathogens. These pathogens also enter the host's body when the tick begins to suck blood. The tick sprays a little saliva into the skin to anesthetize the area and slow the flow of blood. If the tick is infected, depending on which stowaways it's carrying, it will inject bacteria and viruses when it pierces the skin. And then things get unpleasant for the person who has been bitten.

What can happen? If the pathogen is a bacterium, it will be *Borrelia*, the spiral-shaped culprit behind many tick-borne diseases, including Lyme disease. Although Lyme disease was first isolated in Lyme, Connecticut, where it got its name, it has since spread to other parts of North America. In many cases, your body will deal with the intruder. But often that doesn't happen, and it begins its dastardly work. If you're lucky, a red ring resembling a target with the bite as the bull's eye will betray its presence. If you're lucky? Yes, it really is lucky because then you know you have an acute infection. A visit to your family doctor, a course of antibiotics for a few days, and everything will be okay.

And what happens if there is no red ring? Then you don't know. Either your body has managed just fine on its own, or you are not infected. If the tick was on your skin for only a few hours, it probably didn't have a chance to start sucking. Should you go to the doctor all the same? The doctor will need to take a blood sample as that will be the only way to know for sure if the bacteria in question is in your system. People who spend a lot of time outdoors can't go to the doctor every time they get a tick bite. I'll tell you how I deal with it. Every time I go to the doctor for some other reason (for instance, a check-up) and the doctor orders blood drawn anyway, I ask to be tested for *Borrelia*. Apart from that, it's a good idea to get checked out in the fall. When temperatures drop, ticks take a break. If you live in a place with frosty winters, you can happily hike through the cold season without worrying about ticks.

Those of you who encounter ticks regularly probably have blood profiles like mine: the level of antibodies is always high, which usually would be a cause for concern. I say usually, because an immunological trace in your blood doesn't necessarily mean you currently have an infection. It could simply mean your body has successfully overcome infections in the past. As I have never had further symptoms, my family doctor thought I might be one of the lucky few whose body can deal with *Borrelia* on its own. But then one day I began to get severe headaches that lasted for a week or more. I began to suspect I might have an infection after all. A special blood test confirmed my suspicion. The dreaded spiral bacteria were wreaking havoc inside me.

There was only one thing to do: begin a months-long course of antibiotics. Luckily, I tolerated the drugs well, and the treatment succeeded. Since then the sight of ticks has troubled me more because, unfortunately, you don't develop an immunity. There's no vaccination in sight, either, because there's a whole range of different *Borrelia* that could infect you. And the symptoms are not necessarily restricted to headaches. At later stages there could also be inflammation of the nervous system, which could lead to Bell's palsy, for instance, or extreme joint pain. When the attacking organism has advanced this far into the body, treatment can become difficult. And so, as soon as you suspect you have unusual symptoms after a tick bite, you should go to a doctor.

The U.S.-based Centers for Disease Control and Prevention publish an extensive website that discusses the dangers posed by ticks and provides a map showing their distribution in the United States, and the Government of Canada also publishes maps showing the risks of contracting Lyme disease from ticks across the country. Increased forest fragmentation, housing developments that provide habitat for mice (another important host for ticks), and large deer populations mean disease-infected ticks will become more common and widespread in the future. Small mammals are our friends when it comes to ticks. Well, not the mice that host them, but the raccoons that eat the mice and the possums that eat the ticks.

Ticks are likely the most unpleasant but, unfortunately, not the only pesky critters you might encounter on your forest walks. Mosquitoes and midges love moist air. When the summer sun rises over dew-bedecked meadows, these little devils are in their element. They don't like dry air and shimmering summer heat, and the forest provides a place where they can avoid both. Here the air is noticeably more humid, and eternal shade rules. If you're hiking in a rainy year and in need of a place to rest, don't search for one deep in the forest. Instead, find a place at the edge of a clearing. Under the first row of trees you will experience the drier air of the clearing and yet still enjoy the shade. A windy spot is even better, because the little fliers avoid them like the plague. They can't reliably zero in on their victims when they're constantly getting blown off track. Time of day is also important. In the morning and evening, the sun is weak and the air correspondingly moister. Around noon, in contrast, you get the hot, dry conditions mosquitoes and their ilk hate most, except for inside the forest, which these insects find especially attractive after a rain shower. Avoid washing your hair just before going for a hike. Mosquitoes and midges are drawn by the smell of fresh shampoo and will dive-bomb your scalp. If you don't want to go out and about with unwashed hair, put on a hat (which will, of course, immediately ruin your coiffure).

And then there are horseflies and the slightly smaller but no less voracious deerflies. Annoyingly enough, these large biting flies prefer conditions exactly opposite to those enjoyed by mosquitoes and midges: they most like to fly in the heat of the midday sun. Therefore, if you've fled from the darkness of the woods into the open to escape mosquitoes, you might find these flies waiting to greet you. I experienced horsefly hospitality on a hike with my brother in Germany's Eifel National Park. The weather was perfect, and the trail meandered most delightfully by a stream with meadows on either side. But along one section of the trail, the horseflies attacked my brother so relentlessly for a distance of several miles that we had to call off our hike. And horseflies are vicious. Okay, I know they can't do anything about their innate behavior, but you must be an extreme nature lover not to take offense at their incessant aerial approaches followed by a soft touchdown and a painful bite. If you have the choice between the lesser of two evils, in this case mosquitoes and the large biting flies, I suggest you choose mosquitoes. And so, take refuge deep in the forest. Horseflies and deerflies detest shade and you will soon be rid of them.

If you can't choose your route (for example, if you're hiking in a group and the leader hasn't thought of details such as the environmental preferences of biting flies), sturdy clothes might improve your hiking experience. Outdoor clothing manufacturers offer shirts, blouses, and pants made of fabric thick enough to be guaranteed bug proof. I had plenty of opportunity to test these out on my trips to Lapland: the shirts and pants worked as advertised. Despite that, after a long day of hiking through the mountains I still ended up with about forty bites from enormous midges (much larger than the ones I am used to in Germany). The weak spot in my defenses, however, was not the fabric but the fact that every time I sat down, my pant legs rose up, exposing my socks. The insects noticed immediately and bit me through the loops of black wool. Jane, who often hikes in the heat, prefers loose, baggy clothing that leaves a gap between the fabric and your skin. That way even if a fly lands with the intention of biting you, it will (hopefully!) find nothing but air where it expected to pierce some nice, firm flesh.

Other bug-fighting options are chemical. You can spray products not only on exposed skin but also, if necessary, on your hair and any clothing that isn't bite proof. But be careful. Some preparations dissolve fabric, which means material made from certain fibers can break down. Not only that but compounds such as DEET (Diethyl-meta-toluamide) don't just get on mosquitoes' nerves, they might also get on yours— literally. They penetrate easily through the skin and enter your bloodstream, where they reach your central nervous system. Tingling and numbness are the least of your worries. They are also suspected of causing damage to brain cells. Less harmful are preparations made purely from plant products, such as cedarwood oil. You soon get used to the penetrating odor, but so do the mosquitoes. As the deterrent effect of this pungent oil is limited to a few hours, you need to reapply it often.

So, where does that leave us? This is what I do. First, I wear mosquito-proof clothing and then I apply a chemical product (only to the most vulnerable areas, around the socks, hands, face, and neck) that consumer testing has proven to be both effective and relatively benign. If the problem is confined to mosquitoes and doesn't include the larger biting flies and ticks, the breeze you create simply by walking will keep them away. You will have to deal with attacks only when you rest for an extended period and you can plan how best to fight back then.

Other delightful creatures you might encounter are chiggers and a whole host of other no-see-ums (otherwise known as midges). Chiggers are mites, which puts them in the same family as ticks and spiders. They are active when ground temperatures are between 77- and 88-degrees Fahrenheit (25 to 30 degrees Celsius) and they die when temperatures dip below 42 degrees Fahrenheit (6 degrees Celsius). They are so tiny you cannot see them unless you happen to have a magnifying glass to hand, which you might if you are going into the forest to check out what is crawling around in the leaf litter.

Chigger larvae bite, and their bites stay annoyingly itchy for a few days. If you give in and scratch, the resulting rash can last a week or two. Chiggers, like ticks, hang out on leaves and grass close to the ground just waiting for you to pass by so they can hitch a ride. Take the same precautions as for ticks: tuck long pants into socks and use insect repellents. Taking a hot shower helps remove any hitchhikers and if you have been sitting on a picnic blanket, wash that in hot water, as well. Thankfully, chigger bites pose no risk unless you scratch so hard that you get an infection. That said, their bites are extremely annoying. Cold compresses and anti-itch creams will help make them more bearable. No-see-ums (any type of midge) have the annoying habit of flying around your head and the best protection I can recommend are those fetchingly fashionable insect nets you wear over your hat and face.

~ 21 ~

Getting Creative

CAN YOU TELL whether the forest you are walking through is old or new? As Jane discovered when touring forests around North America, the vast majority are no more than one hundred years old. As early as the seventeenth century, the tall, straight, white pines from the Adirondack Mountains in New York State were highly prized for ships' masts and timbers for the British Navy. The tallest and straightest trees were identified with the "king's mark" (three hatchet slashes) to set them aside for use by the British Crown. The following century, white pines in the territory of the Algonquin People in what is now Ontario went to build British navy ships during the Napoleonic Wars. In the nineteenth century, forests in Florida and Texas fueled industrial growth in American cities along the East Coast. Forests that escaped most of those depredations were cut down to fuel the war machine during World War II. At the time, people thought the forests would never end. But then they did.

On the Bruce Peninsula in Ontario, which today has the largest remaining area of forest in southern Ontario, it took less than twenty years after the first sawmill arrived in

1881 for the most valuable trees to disappear. By the mid-1920s, so many trees had been cut down that you could see clear from one side of the peninsula to the other (about twenty-four miles or nearly forty kilometers). Imagine what Henry David Thoreau must have felt in Massachusetts in the mid-1800s as he retreated to his isolated cabin in the woods at Walden Pond with a sense of dread that the mighty trees he so admired would, inevitably, fall to the lumberjack's ax.

Some fragments of forest remained uncut because they were hard to access, because extraordinary individuals owned them, or because conservation groups fought to preserve them. Cook Forest State Park, a remnant of old growth in the Allegheny Mountains in Pennsylvania, survived because the timber-cutting family that owned it believed strongly that parts of the forest should be preserved, including a patch of ancient trees growing tantalizingly close to their sawmill. Pioneer Mothers Memorial Forest in Indiana, where the trees have barely been touched since the early 1800s, was preserved after a community fundraising effort protected it from logging.

It is difficult to imagine what some of the forests we see today would have looked like in the early twentieth century with most of their trees cut down. Even areas touted today as old growth, such as Big Thicket National Preserve in Texas or Congaree National Park in South Carolina, have a history of logging and other human impacts. In Congaree (the largest intact hardwood bottomland forest left in the United States), you can see remnants of the dikes built to protect land from the river's floodwaters in the days when plantation owners tried growing cotton and corn in what had been forest and of mounds the ranchers built so they had somewhere to drive their stock when the river flooded the pastures they had wrested from the trees.

If you've walked through a forest in New England, you will have seen the stone walls running through them. This is not some ancient system of forest fencing but evidence that these forests were once cleared for croplands and pastures that were abandoned when the economy of the area changed. And every so often, you will come across a tree with wide-spreading branches that stands out from the others. Why is it so much larger than the trees growing around it? This is a so-called wolf tree, left to grow in a corner of the pasture to provide shade for the animals. Because it once stood all alone, it could stretch out its branches in the sun. Now that the forest has grown in, its height and wide shape set it apart from the other trees. Gnarled, misshapen apple trees provide another sign that the forest you are walking in has reclaimed a pasture where sheep and cattle once grazed. An apple tree has no thorns to stop animals from eating it, so it stands there stoically as they munch on its fruit and break its branches. The tree ends up contorted and twisted. When the livestock leave, the tree can grow more freely, but its lower trunk and branches remain dense and stunted.

In areas where forests once grew, whether on the East Coast or West Coast or many places in between, the forest is always waiting to return. Birds eat the blue berries of eastern red cedar, then choose a vantage point for their song, excreting the seeds as they perch on gravestones or tall posts. And the trees start to grow. Jane is forever pulling up Douglas fir seedlings that have sprouted in her yard after the wind has blown seeds in from the forest across the street. If she left them alone, she would soon need a machete to make it to her front door. Timber companies, eager for a quick return, get a step up on this process and replant forests they've clear-cut with commercially desirable species, cutting and burning trees that for them have no value and applying herbicides to make sure they stay away.

You can easily figure out whether you are walking in a planted forest or a halfway natural forest that has made some planting decisions of its own by looking for a couple of telltale signs. Let's state the most obvious one first: whether the trees are growing in rows. When Nature is doing the planting, trees never grow in straight lines. Only systematic foresters plant trees that way. Even though it makes no difference in principle how seedlings are planted, foresters like things to be orderly and precise. I learned this early on in my forest service career. First, markers are put out in tree-free areas. These red-and-white poles, about six-and-a-half feet (nearly two meters) tall, are rammed into the ground in a line. Now you can use the markers to get your bearings and plant the little trees in a straight line. And because the trees don't move from the spot where they were planted, decades later you can still make out the rows, unless the timber has been harvested and the forest severely thinned.

A second telltale sign is the species of trees growing in the forest. And I don't mean whether the trees are native to the region or not. The issue is species diversity. If you find single species of deciduous trees in a forest on the East Coast or monoculture of native Douglas firs in the Pacific Northwest, it is unlikely the trees grew naturally. In the same way teak or mahogany plantations are a poor substitute for the diversity of a true tropical rainforest, plantations of oak, beech, or Douglas fir make poor replacements for a primeval forest.

Diversity doesn't just concern species; it is also about age. When large swaths of trees are clear-cut and the replacement trees are all planted at the same time, it's not only hard on the trees but also on the animals and plants that call the forests home and rely on a mix of trees of diverse ages for their food and accommodations. Conditions are slightly better in selectively harvested plantations where a full range of ages grow and where the next generations sprout from seeds dropped from the parent trees. Commercial forests left to develop according to natural cycles can mimic Nature quite closely even when an old tree is cut down occasionally and removed. The only forest indicators you hardly ever find in a stand of trees managed in this way are truly ancient trees or snags. In our modern world, a combination of carefully managed forests and protected areas where trees age naturally represent a good compromise. Unfortunately, such harmonious combinations are hard to find.

In these days when forests increasingly must pay their way to survive, we sometimes must reach for creative solutions. I want to share with you a story from the forest I manage in Germany. Some years ago, the state forest agency planned to log the ancient beeches and replace them with the non-native Douglas firs favored by the German timber industry. In ancient times, Germany was almost completely covered in beech forest. Today, less than a tenth of a percent of these old trees remains. The community I now work for, Hümmel, owned about 250 acres (100 hectares) of this precious resource, and I wanted to keep it that way. One day over a beer with friends I laughed about another community where foresters were burying urns in the forest. The forester-turned-undertaker was selling the ancient beeches as living grave markers. It seemed a preposterous idea, and yet... And so it was we set up our burial forest in Hümmel.

People can reserve a spot under their favorite tree. When the time comes, the biodegradable urn containing their ashes is buried. The family holds whatever kind of service they like. We had one celebration where the family brought a keg of beer and poured a glass for everyone present. Afterward the spot is covered over and left to look like any other spot in the forest. The only marker is a small metal plate on the tree engraved with the names of the people buried beside it. Families who come to visit their loved ones have picnics in the forest, children and dogs play, people take a walk. One man, in a gesture I find particularly moving, came every year with hearts he made at home out of ice, so he could take them to his wife's grave and let them melt in the sun, leaving no trace of their passing. And so, our old-growth forest was protected.

Memorial forests are catching on in North America. Jane visited a cemetery in Ontario that has recently created a natural burial ground in a section of woodland on the property, and there are private forests where you can schedule a visit to choose a tree where you would like your ashes returned to nature. Joan Maloof, founder of the Old-Growth Forest Network, established a September 11th Memorial Forest near her home to protect a stand of old trees from being cleared to create a public park.

Apart from the fact that more and larger forested areas should be protected, there's nothing intrinsically bad about using wood. This natural material brings a little of the forest into our homes. The modern fashion for wooden furniture is an example. Manufacturers now intentionally incorporate imperfections once considered unacceptable: fat knots, color variations, spiral patterns, or even wormholes. The more there are, the more distinctive and original the furniture. There is even a finish that enhances growth rings until you can feel them, making your tabletop or work surface distinctively tactile and revealing the conditions the tree has endured over the course of its life.

If the tree has grown up without incident, when its trunk is sawn into boards along its length, the annual growth rings show up as longitudinal stripes. But when things have gone awry, you'll see spiral patterns. These result from the repairs the tree has undertaken and the extra growing it had to do to keep its equilibrium. For example, if a pine grew crooked in its youth and later straightened itself out by growing more wood on one side, the stripes will angle through the boards. Sometimes more direct damage drives a tree to grow its wood in unusual patterns. Perhaps a neighboring tree felled by a storm ripped some of the bark off its companion, causing a deep gash. To prevent wood-eating fungi from penetrating the wound, the damaged tree attempted to grow wood quickly to seal off this area and a woody lump formed. Depending on the size of the wound, this swelling could be very large. Bad news for the tree, but good news for the woodworker: the patterns in the tabletop fashioned from this wood will be especially varied.

Even knots in the wood say something about the life the tree has led. Knots show where branches grew. If the knots are the same color as the surrounding wood, the branches were still green when the tree was cut down. That is to say they were still alive. Knots like these are solidly attached to the surrounding wood and disrupt neither its aesthetic appeal (although that might be a matter of personal taste) nor the durability of the piece of wood. It's a different matter with knots that are darker around the edges or all the way through. These knots were left by dead branches, and the tree would have been in the process of growing new wood to seal off the branch stub. Often the base of the branch is not surrounded by new, healthy wood, which means the tree was harvested before it had a chance to finish its repair work.

If the dark knot is completely circular when you look down on it, the board was cut crosswise to the direction of growth. And because the branch was already dead, the knot is only loosely attached to the surrounding woody tissue. If the board dries out, the circular knot will shrink at a different rate from the surrounding wood and fall out, resulting in the famous knothole that you can peek through. That can be fun if it's not in furniture or floorboards. If a knot falls out in a high-quality woodshop during the production process, the woodworker will fill the hole with a plug of the same type of wood so you can hardly tell the hole was there.

Floorboards or furniture with no knots have usually been made from particularly massive, ancient trees. These lost their dead branches (which they no longer needed below their crowns) and finished walling off the base of these branches with thick layers of new wood long before they were harvested. These knot-free products command high prices.

With the choice of wood out there these days, you can even specify whether you want your furniture to be made from old or young trees. People used to want their beech-wood light in color and free from imperfections. Stands over 140 years old were less valuable because as beeches age, their inner wood takes on a reddish tinge. Boards made from red-heart beech are not uniform in color and the discrepancies range from slight color variations to fiery red patterns. For some years now, in response to the suggestions of foresters, the furniture industry has marketed red-heart beech as wild beech or heart beech. The rebranding worked, and customers love the distinctively patterned wood. And because they do, beeches can stay standing in the forest for a few more decades to mature. Birds can build their nests in their mighty crowns, and woodpeckers can carve out the occasional cavity. And because individual trees die as they get older, the amount of deadwood in these stands of elderly beeches increases. If you want to help birds, insects, and fungi, choose red-heart beech.

You can make even more of a difference if you buy your tables and chairs from a local carpenter, with the added advantage that you can treasure these pieces of craftsmanship. I had my new desk made by just such a small undertaking and, I admit, that was purely happenstance. I am about six-and-a-half feet (two meters) tall and none of the desks made by the large furniture chains fit me. There was nothing for it: I had to have one custom made to spare my back. Employees at a small enterprise enrolled in one of my seminars. The name of the business immediately caught my attention: *Holzgespür*. One way of translating this into English would be Wood Sense.

This shop involves clients from the beginning. I got to choose from locally sourced tree trunks. Would I prefer a lively pattern in the growth rings or precise, straight lines? Did I want lots of knots to add interest to the finished desktop? To make the choice easier, the owner sent me a short video so I could make a virtual visit to the workshop and thoroughly examine my tree. They kept me well informed on the progress of my desk. When this wonderful piece was finally installed in my office, I was overjoyed. My desk exceeded my expectations. Such enterprises exist in North America, as well, where craftspeople work with small-scale, local loggers to find special pieces of wood they can fashion into furniture that reflects the region of its making.

Of course, a custom-made desk costs more than one you pick up at a discount furniture outlet; however, the solid construction and timeless organic design mean you end up with a piece you can pass down for generations. This move away from cheap objects we throw away benefits the forest, because it means that, in the end, we use less wood.

And trees that might otherwise be discarded, burned, or left to rot are not just being turned into furniture. Earlier I mentioned the live-oak crooks at Mystic Seaport in Connecticut waiting to be incorporated in the structures of wooden boats. Up in the Pacific Northwest, boatbuilder Jay Smith of Fidalgo Island, Washington, sourced misfits of wood from Oregon loggers so he could build *Polaris*, a thirty-six-foot (eleven-meter) replica of a Viking longboat, which was pulled by four heavy horses and launched in Bowman Bay, near Anacortes, in 2017—ancient trees finding new life on the world's oceans.

Carolina wren, Poinsett State Park, South Carolina

In Closing

THIS BOOK IS not a reference book. It's an appetizer. You won't have taken note of, and don't need to have taken note of, all the things I've talked about. Perhaps you've dipped in here and there to read more about things you've experienced in the forest. Much more important than the contents of this book are the gifts you have already: your eyes, ears, nose, and tongue. You have the perfect tools to undertake an exciting adventure into the forests right outside your front door. The forests out there are yours, and they are just waiting for you to discover them. Go out and enjoy. Tread the paths lightly and leave everything just as you found it. I wish you much joy in discoveries both large and small. If this little book has inspired you to go out hiking in the woods, then I have achieved my goal.

NOTES

1: TOTAL IMMERSION

Leaves and needles whisper and sing For more on the sounds made by different types of wood, see Vincent Wozniak O'Connor, "Silviphonics: Sound in Timber" in *Materials of Sound, Journal of Sonic Studies* 16 (2018).

In spring, pines pump more terpenes Marco Michelozzi, "Defensive Roles of Terpenoid Mixtures in Conifers," *Acta Botanica Gallica*, 146, no. 1 (1999): 73–84, https://dx.doi.org/10.1080/12538078.1999.10515803.

Conifers use terpenes in other ways J. G. Slowik, C. Stroud, J. W. Bottenheim, et al., "Characterization of a Large Biogenic Secondary Organic Aerosol Event from Eastern Canadian Forests," *Atmospheric Chemistry and Physics* 10, no. 6 (2010): 2825–2845, https://doi.org/10.5194/acp-10-2825-2010.

Scientists at the University of Tel Aviv Marine Veits, Itzhak Khait, Uri Obolski, et al., "Flowers Respond to Pollinator Sound Within Minutes by Increasing Nectar Sugar Concentration," *Ecology Letters* 22, no. 9 (July 2019): 1483–1492, https://doi.org/10.1111/ele.13331.

2: THE ROOT OF THE MATTER

Baldcypress trees grow "knees" For more on baldcypress knees, see Christopher H. Briand, "Cypress Knees: An Enduring Enigma," *Arnoldia (Jamaica Plain)* 60, no. 4 (2000): 19–25.

Nutrients are hard to come by, so the thrifty red spruces engineer an
ecosystem For more on how red spruce engineer their ecosystems,
see Steven L. Stephenson, *A Natural History of the Appalachians*
(Morgantown: West Virginia University Press, 2013), page 60.

3: WHAT THE TREES CAN TELL YOU

In Algonquin Provincial Park in Ontario, Canada The Friends of
Algonquin Park publish an excellent series of booklets on the park's
many trails. See Dan Strickland, "Post 8: The Big Question About the
Big Pine" in *Big Pines Trail* (Whitney, ON: The Friends of Algonquin
Park, nd).

In an ancient forest of eastern white cedar on the Niagara Escarpment For
more on these cedars, see Peter E. Kelly and Douglas W. Larson, *The
Last Stand: A Journey Through the Ancient Cliff-Face Forest of the Niagara
Escarpment* (Toronto: Natural Heritage Books, 2007).

*In Harvard Forest, an ecological research area in Petersham, Massachusetts,
a large white pine with a curved trunk* You can take a virtual tour of
the French Road Trail (and other trails in the Harvard experimental
forest) by visiting https://harvardforest.fas.harvard.edu/trails-
recreation. The tilted pine can be found at stop 4, "Land-Use Legacies."

Multiple trunks can also be a sign of human activity in the forest For
more on how human activity affects the form of trees in forests, see
Tom Wessels, *Reading the Forested Landscape: A Natural History of New
England* (Woodstock, VT: The Countryman Press, 1997). Coppicing is
mentioned on page 26.

Some of the redwoods in southern Oregon For more on redwood burls,
see Peter Del Tredici, "Redwood Burls: Immortality Underground,"
Arnoldia (Jamaica Plain) 59, no. 3 (1999): 14–22.

Even when trunks grow mostly straight Hans Kubler, "Function of Spiral
Grain in Trees," *Trees* 5, no. 3 (1991): 125–135, https://doi.org/10.1007/
BF00204333.

4: LEAVES, NUTS, AND SEEDS

When a tree is cut down and milled into lumber For information on how
trees shed their branches see this article by Chittenden (Vermont)
County Forester Michael Snyder: "Wood Whys: Self-Pruning Branches,"
Northern Woodlands (Spring 2015).

Because leaf production is all about light The Virtual Nature Trail at Penn State New Kensington in western Pennsylvania managed by Pennsylvania State University is another virtual forest trail you can enjoy from the comfort of your own home. For more on leaves and light, see the section "Leaf Shapes and Strategies" at https://www.psu.edu/dept/nkbiology/naturetrail/leaves.htm.

Understory trees such as dogwoods Henry S. Horn, *The Adaptive Geometry of Trees* (Princeton, NJ: Princeton University Press, 1971), page 114.

That small red thing on a yew that Jane always thought was a fruit There are many great options for taking informative nature walks online. Here is one from Yale University that explains the arils on yews (that's the scientific name for the red pseudofruits). This is an urban nature walk in the area around the Yale University campus in New Haven, Connecticut, and the details about yews can be found at https://naturewalk.yale.edu/trees/taxaceae/taxus-x-media/yew-38.

According to ornithologist and author John K. Terres Eldon Greij, "Why Mallards and Other Birds Have No Teeth and Sometimes Eat Pebbles," *BirdWatching.* Originally published in the column "Amazing Birds" November/December 2014, updated October 4, 2018, https://www.birdwatchingdaily.com/news/science/why-mallards-and-other-birds-have-no-teeth-and-sometimes-eat-pebbles/.

Acorn woodpeckers in oak forests peck holes in standing dead trees For more cool facts on acorn woodpeckers, enjoy Matthew L. Miller's April 24, 2017, article "Acorn Woodpecker: The Fascinating Life of the Master Hoarder" on the Nature Conservancy's webpage *Cool Green Science,* https://blog.nature.org/science/2017/04/24/acorn-woodpecker-the-fascinating-life-of-the-master-hoarder/.

5: THE BEAUTY OF BARK

The nature writer and conservationist known as Grey Owl For more on Grey Owl, see Donald B. Smith "Archibald Belaney, Grey Owl," *The Canadian Encyclopedia* online, https://www.thecanadianencyclopedia.ca/en/article/archibald-belaney-grey-owl.

The "church door" or "cat face," as foresters sometimes call it Dan Strickland, "Post 11: The Big Pines and the Big Picture," *Big Pines Trail* (Whitney, ON: The Friends of Algonquin Park, n.d.).

Jane came across an example of this on a magnificent white pine Dan Strickland, "Post 8: The Big Question About the Big Pine," *Big Pines Trail* (Whitney, ON: The Friends of Algonquin Park, n.d.).

Frost ribs provide further evidence Frost ribs are described and illustrated in Michael Wojtech, *Bark: A Field Guide to Trees of the Northeast* (Hanover and London: University Press of New England, 2011), pages 66–67.

6: HITCHING A RIDE OR PAYING THE RENT?

Dwarf mistletoe in the forests of the Pacific Northwest United States Department of Agriculture, US Forest Service Research and Development, "Dwarf Mistletoe," https://www.fs.fed.us/research/ invasive-species/plant-pathogens/dwarf-mistletoe.php.

The trees in ancient forests in the Pacific Northwest Jon R. Luoma, *The Hidden Forest: The Biography of an Ecosystem* (Corvallis: Oregon State University Press, 1999), pages 52–57 and page 69.

Ferns using trees to hitch a ride to the sun For more on life in the redwood canopy, see Stephen S. Sillett and Robert Van Pelt, "A Redwood Tree Whose Crown Is a Forest Canopy," *Northwest Science* 74, no. 1 (2000): 34–43.

Live oaks in southern forests are covered with a fascinating plant called the resurrection fern You can read more about the properties of these amazing ferns in Christopher Krieg and Sandy Saunders, "Ferns in Space," *Palmetto* 33, no. 2 (2016): 8–10.

In 1984, researchers in Antarctica dug out moss that had been frozen Esme Roads, Royce E. Longton, and Peter Convey, "Millennial Timescale Regeneration in a Moss from Antarctica," *Current Biology* 24, no. 6 (March 17, 2014): R222–R223, https://doi.org/10.1016/j. cub.2014.01.053.

Tardigrades, commonly known as water bears or moss piglets S. Hengherr, M. R. Worland, A. Reuner, et al., "Freeze Tolerance, Supercooling Points and Ice Formation: Comparative Studies on the Subzero Temperature Survival of Limno-Terrestrial Tardigrades," *Journal of Experimental Biology* 212, no. 6 (2009): 802–807, https://doi.org/10.1242/jeb.025973.

If you examine mosses up close The wonderful world of mosses is covered in detail in Robin Wall Kimmerer's delightful book *Gathering*

Moss: A Natural and Cultural History of Mosses (Corvallis: Oregon State University Press, 2003).

A moss in a Hawaiian forest Eric F. Karlin, Sara C. Hotchkiss, Sandra B. Boles, et al., "High Genetic Diversity in a Remote Island Population System: Sans Sex," *New Phytologist* 193, no. 4 (2011): 1088–1097, https://doi.org/10.1111/j.1469-8137.2011.03999.x.

The moss coating on the forest floor Jed Cappellazzi, "The Influence of Forest Floor Moss Cover on Ectomycorrhizal Abundance in the Central-Western Orgon Cascade Mountains" (Bachelor of Science, Oregon State, 2007), https://andrewsforest.oregonstate.edu/sites/default/files/lter/pubs/pdf/pub4336.pdf.

7: THE IMPORTANCE OF DECAY

Tree-ring scientists gather data by drilling Jim Robbins, "Chronicles of the Rings: What Trees Tell Us," *New York Times*, April 30, 2019, https://www.nytimes.com/2019/04/30/science/tree-rings-climate.html.

Using this method, researchers from the Tree-Ring Laboratory D. W. Stahle, J. R. Edmondson, I. M. Howard, et al., "Longevity, Climate Sensitivity, and Conservation Status of Wetland Trees at Black River, North Carolina," *Environmental Research Communications* 1, no. 4 (2019), https://doi.org/10.1088/2515-7620/ab0c4a.

How the stump is rotting Tom Wessels, *Reading the Forested Landscape: A Natural History of New England* (Woodstock, VT: The Countryman Press, 1997), pages 66–67.

Interestingly, these little nocturnal frogs can survive being frozen J. R. Layne Jr. and A. L. Jones, "Freeze Tolerance in the Gray Treefrog: Cryoprotectant Mobilization and Organ Dehydration," *Journal of Experimental Zoology* 290, no. 1 (June 15, 2001): 1–5.

Given the choice between fixing a silent leak Lars Wilsson, *My Beaver Colony* (New York: Doubleday, 1968).

If you hear a weird whirring, thrumming sound in a northern forest Carrie L. Schumacher, Craig A. Harper, David A. Buehler, et al., "Drumming Log Habitat Selection by Male Ruffed Grouse in North Carolina," *Proceedings of the Annual Conference of the Southeast Association of Fish and Wildlife Agencies* 55 (2001): 466–474.

8: SPOTLIGHT ON THE DECOMPOSERS

The forests adapted to their new maintenance crew and today earthworms are considered invasive Lee E. Frelich, Cindy M. Hale, Stefan Scheu, et al., "Earthworm Invasion into Previously Earthworm-Free Temperate and Boreal Forests," *Biological Invasions* 8, no. 6 (2006): 1235–1245, https://doi.org/10.1007/s10530-006-9019-3.

There can be as many as two thousand earthworms Blake Eligh, "Invasive Earthworms Are Eating Away at Forest Diversity: U of T Study," press release, University of Toronto, May 5, 2016, https://www.utoronto.ca/news/invasive-earthworms-are-eating-away-forest-diversity-u-t-study.

This technique of attracting worms to the surface even has a name: worm grunting O. Mitra, M. A. Callaham, M. L. Smith, and J. E. Yack, "Grunting for Worms: Seismic Vibrations Cause *Diplocardia* Earthworms to Emerge From the Soil," *Biology Letters* 5, no. 1 (October 21, 2008): 16–19, https://doi.org/10.1098/rsbl.2008.0456.

Ants in Vermont forests Aaron M. Gotelli and Nicholas J. Ellison, *A Field Guide to the Ants of New England* (New Haven: Yale University Press, 2012).

Millipedes like dark, moist places Atlas Obscura, "Glowing Millipedes of Sequoia National Park," https://www.atlasobscura.com/places/glowing-millipedes-of-sequoia-national-park.

You could think of a fungal thread as a sort of inside-out digestive system Kevin Garcia and Sabine D. Zimmermann, "The Role of Mycorrhizal Associations in Plant Potassium Nutrition," *Frontiers in Plant Science* 5 (July 17, 2014): 337, https:// doi.org/10.3389/fpls.2014.00337.

The largest fungus found so far For more on this amazing fungus, see Craig L. Schmitt and Michael Tatum, *The Malheur National Forest: Location of the World's Largest Living Organism (The Humongous Fungus)*, (United States Department of Agriculture: Forest Service Pacific Northwest Region, 2008): 4.

One of the most fascinating aspects of banana slugs is their slime For more on this fascinating subject, see Sarah McQuate, "He Slimed Me!" guest blog, *Scientific American*, December 7, 2016, https://blogs.scientificamerican.com/guest-blog/he-slimed-me/.

Notes

9: INTERPRETING THE FOREST FOR CHILDREN

As you're snapping twigs open Twigs contain a wealth of interesting details. To explore further, see Kim D. Coder, "Describing Twigs," Tree Anatomy Series, Warnell School of Forestry and Natural Resources 14-22, November 2014, https://www.warnell.uga.edu/sites/default/files/publications/Tree%20Anatomy%20Describing%20Twigs_14-22.pdf.

10: FOREST ACTIVITIES WITH CHILDREN

Researchers in the Santa Cruz Mountains in California Justin P. Suraci, Michael Clinchy, Liana Y. Zanette, and Christopher C. Wilmers, "Fear of Humans as Apex Predators Has Landscape-Scale Impacts From Mountain Lions to Mice," *Ecology Letters* 22, no. 10 (July 17, 2019): 1578–1586, https://doi.org/10.1111/ele.13344.

As you get to know the forest better The USA National Phenology Network has a project called Nature's Notebook, which gives you pointers on setting up your own nature-tracking program. Or you could join with other contributors at iNaturalist to help identify what you see and share and discuss your findings.

11: THE FOREST AT NIGHT

I find a recent scientific discovery especially touching: trees fall asleep Eetu Puttonnen, Christian Briese, Gottfried Mandlburger, et al., "Quantification of Overnight Movement of Birch *(Betula pendula)* Branches and Foliage with Short Interval Terrestrial Laser Scanning," *Frontiers of Plant Science* 7 (February 29, 2016): 222, https://doi.org/10.3389/fpls.2016.00222.

Scientists have also recently discovered that it takes a while for plants to adjust to light Avichai Tendler, Bat Chen Wolf, Vivekanand Tiwari, et al., "Fold-Change Response of Photosynthesis to Step Increases of Light Level," *iScience* 8 (October 26, 2018): 126–137, https://doi.org/10.1016/j.isci.2018.09.019.

Another process you won't notice is that trees get fatter at night Martina Huber, "Forscher schauen 300 Bäume beim Wachsen zu" [Researchers watch 300 trees grow], *Tierwelt* 3 (July 4, 2016): 24–25.

A firefly's light is the product of a chemical reaction Annick Bay and Jean Pol Vigneron, "Light Extraction From the Bioluminescent

Organs of Fireflies," Proceedings of SPIE (International Society for Optical Engineering) *Biomimetics and Bioinspiration*, 740108 (August 21, 2009), https://doi.org/10.1117/12.825473.

Recent research has revealed that flying squirrels turn bubblegum pink Meilan Solly, "Flying Squirrels Glow Fluorescent Pink Under Ultraviolet Light," *Smithsonian* magazine, February 1, 2019, https://www.smithsonianmag.com/smart-news/flying-squirrels-glow-fluorescent-pink-under-ultraviolet-light-180971397/.

The wings of the northern saw-whet owl Cara Giaimo, "Everything We Know About Birds That Glow," *Atlas Obscura*, April 11, 2018, https://www.atlasobscura.com/articles/why-birds-glow-blacklight.

You likely won't be lucky enough to spot a flying squirrel but, if you are in the South, you might find a scorpion For fun facts about glow-in-the-dark scorpions, see C. Claiborne Ray, "The Mystery of a Scorpion's Glow," *New York Times*, December 4, 2017, https://www.nytimes.com/2017/12/04/science/scorpions-fluorescence-ultraviolet.html.

12: SEASONAL WALKS

This hair-like ice is the frozen breath of fungi D. Hofmann, G. Preuss, and C. Mätzler, "Evidence for Biological Shaping of Hair Ice," *Biogeosciences*, 12, no. 14 (July 22, 2015): 4261–4273, https://doi.org/10.5194/bg-12-4261-2015.

Feral pigs find shelter also Andrea Anderson, "Huge Feral Hogs Invading Canada, Building 'Pigloos' as They Go," *National Geographic*, April 3, 2020, https://www.nationalgeographic.com/animals/2020/03/huge-feral-hogs-swine-spreading-through-north-canada/.

13: HIDDEN CONNECTIONS

To understand how populations of predators and prey affect each other For information on Isle Royale, see http://isleroyalewolf.org.

And to do that, we'll travel in our minds to Yellowstone National Park For information on Yellowstone wolf numbers, see Douglas W. Smith, Daniel R. Stahler, and Debra S. Guernsey, *Yellowstone Wolf Project Annual Report 2005* (Yellowstone National Park, Wyoming: Yellowstone Center for Resources, 2005): 2, https://www.nps.gov/yell/learn/nature/upload/wolfrpt05.pdf.

Here's an example you might see in your own backyard Theresa Wei Ying Ong and John H. Vandermeer. "Coupling Unstable Agents in Biological Control," *Nature Communications* 6, no. 1 (2015): 5991, https://doi.org/10.1038/ncomms6991.

Take the spruce budworm in Pacific Northwest forests Torolf R. Torgersen, "Ecological Processes," poster for the United States Department of Agriculture, Forest Service, Pacific Northwest Research Station, n.d., personal collection of Jane Billinghurst.

Take holly trees growing in East Coast forests Vera Krischik, Eric S. McCloud, and John A. Davidson, "Selective Avoidance by Vertebrate Frugivores of Green Holly Berries Infested with a Cecidomyiid Fly (Diptera: Cecidomyiidae)," *The American Midland Naturalist* 121, no. 2 (April 1989): 350–354, https://doi.org/10.2307/2426039.

He called it the spin-dry cycle, which is when dragonflies fly in a spiral pattern James S. Walker, "Spin-Dry Dragonflies" *ARGIA: The News Journal of the Dragonfly Society of the Americas* 23, no. 3 (2011): 29–31.

14: SPOTTING WILDLIFE

Found in southern pine savannahs, fox squirrels live in a three-way relationship For more information on fox squirrels, see Ellie Whitney, D. Bruce Means, and Anne Rudloe, *Priceless Florida: Natural Ecosystems and Native Species* (Sarasota: Pineapple Press, 2004), pages 45–46.

The way squirrels indicate alarm Thaddeus R. McRae and Steven M. Green, "Joint Tail and Vocal Alarm Signals of Gray Squirrels (Sciurus carolinensis)," *Behaviour* 151, no. 10 (September 2, 2014): 1433–1452, https://doi.org/10.1163/1568539X-00003194.

After a forty-year absence, in summer 2019, red-cockaded woodpeckers were nesting United States Department of Agriculture, Forest Service, Francis Marion and Sumter National Forests, "Partnership Restores Red-cockaded Woodpeckers to Sumter National Forest," https://www.fs.usda.gov/detailfull/scnfs/home/?cid=FSEPRD638347&width=full.

15: FINDING BEAUTY IN SMALL THINGS

In roughly ten square feet (one square meter) of an undisturbed forest, there can be as many as one hundred spiders This estimate comes from Rachel Carson, *Silent Spring* (New York: Houghton Mifflin, 1962), where she estimates "a biologically sound forest has 50 to 150 spiders to the square meter."

A lens of about 16X magnification works well There's a good discussion of hand lenses here: Penn State Extension, "A Brief Guide to Hand Lenses," https://extension.psu.edu/a-brief-guide-to-hand-lenses.

In 2019, the Hickory Nut Gorge green salamander Austin Patton, Joseph J. Apodaca, Jeffrey D. Corser, et al., "A New Green Salamander in the Southern Appalachians: Evolutionary History of *Aneides aeneus* and Implications for Management and Conservation with the Description of a Cryptic Microendemic Species," *Copeia* 107, no. 4 (2019): 748–763, https://doi.org/10.1643/CH-18-052.

Foresters value ants in the forest Aaron M. Ellison, "Ants and Trees: A Lifelong Relationship," *American Forests* (winter 2014), https://www.americanforests.org/magazine/article/ants-and-trees-a-lifelong-relationship/.

It has a trunk like an elephant Klara Krämer, Dipl. Biol., RWTH Aachen University, Institute for Environmental Research (Biology V), Chair of Environmental Biology and Chemodynamics (UBC), email correspondence with Peter Wohlleben, March 30, 2016.

20: CHOOSING YOUR WARDROBE

Strictly speaking, deer and feral hogs, like most mammals, see only blue or not-blue Peter K. Ahnelt, "Farbensehen beim Schalenwild: Unterscheidung in Blau und 'Nicht-Blau,'" [Color vision in hoofed game: Distinguishing between blue and not-blue] in *Revierkurier* 3 (2009): 4–5.

"Are there lots of ticks out there?" For more on managing encounters with ticks, see https://tickencounter.org, a site run by the University of Rhode Island, which includes tips on prevention, testing, and identification.

Here is the link to the tick site managed by the Centers for Disease Control and Prevention: https://www.cdc.gov/ticks/index.html.

Here is the link to information from the Government of Canada on the prevalence of tick in that country: https://www.canada.ca/en/public-health/services/diseases/lyme-disease/risk-lyme-disease.html.

21: GETTING CREATIVE

In Congaree (the largest intact hardwood bottomland forest left in the United States) For more on the regrowth of trees in Congaree National Park, see Mark Kinzer, *Nature's Return: An Environmental History of Congaree National Park* (Columbia: South Carolina Press, 2017). *September 11th Memorial Forest* Joan Maloof, *Teaching the Trees* (Athens: University of Georgia Press, 2005): 120.

Even knots in the wood say something about the life the tree has led This article by Chittenden (Vermont) County Forester Michael Snyder explains more about knots in lumber and how foresters maintain forests to minimize them: "What is the Difference Between Red Knots and Black Knots?" *Northern Woodlands* (Spring 2008).

Earlier I mentioned the live-oak crooks at Mystic Seaport in Connecticut For a beautifully illustrated description of the project and the launch of this replica of a Viking longboat, see Arista Holden, "Polaris: A Viking Ship for Gloucester, Massachusetts," in *WoodenBoat*, https:// www.woodenboat.com/polaris-0.

BIBLIOGRAPHY

Here is a selection of the books and resources that enhanced Jane's appreciation for and understanding of the forests she visited while researching her contributions to this book. Many parks also have excellent handouts, trail guides, and interpretive programs to help you make the most of your visit.

Barton, Andrew M. *The Changing Nature of the Maine Woods*. Durham, New Hampshire: University of New Hampshire Press, 2012.

DiNunzio, Michael G. *Adirondack Wild Guide: A Natural History of the Adirondack Park*. New York: Adirondack Nature Conservancy and The Adirondack Council, 1984.

Global Forest Watch. Interactive forest map. https://globalforest watch.org/map.

Harvard Forest. https://harvardforest.fas.harvard.edu/.

Haskell, David George. *The Forest Unseen: A Year's Watch in Nature*. New York: Penguin, 2012.

Heinrich, Bernd. *The Trees in My Forest*. New York: Cliff Street Books, 1997.

Higgins, Richard. *Thoreau and the Language of Trees*. Oakland: University of California Press, 2017.

Kimmerer, Robin Wall. *Gathering Moss: A Natural and Cultural History of Mosses*. Corvallis: Oregon State University Press, 2003.

Bibliography

Kinzer, Mark. *Nature's Return: An Environment History of Congaree National Park.* Columbia: University of South Carolina Press, 2017.

Luoma, Jon R. *The Hidden Forest: The Biography of an Ecosystem.* Corvallis: Oregon State University Press, 1999.

Maloof, Joan. *Teaching the Trees: Lessons from the Forest.* Athens: University of Georgia Press, 2007.

Maloof, Joan. *Among the Ancients: Adventures in the Eastern Old-Growth Forests.* Washington, DC: Ruka, 2011.

Maloof, Joan. *Nature's Temples: The Complex World of Old-Growth Forests.* Portland, OR: Timber Press, 2016.

Maloof, Joan. *The Living Forest: A Visual Journey into the Heart of the Woods.* Portland, OR: Timber Press, 2017.

Marchand, Peter J. *North Woods: An Inside Look at the Nature of Forests in the Northeast.* Boston: Appalachian Mountain Club, 1987.

Preston, Richard. *The Wild Trees: A Story of Passion and Daring.* New York: Random House, 2007.

Schoettle, Taylor. *A Naturalist's Guide to the Okefenokee Swamp.* Darien, GA: Sea to Sea Printing, 2002.

Stephenson, Steven L. *A Natural History of the Central Appalachians.* Morgantown: West Virginia University Press, 2013.

Thompson, Elizabeth H., and Eric R. Sorenson. *Wetland, Woodland, Wildland: A Guide to the Natural Communities of Vermont.* N.p.: The Nature Conservancy and the Vermont Department of Fish and Wildlife, 2000.

United States Department of Agriculture. *A U.S. Forest Resource Facts and Historical Trends.* Forest Service, FS-1035, August 2014. https://www.fia.fs.fed.us/library/brochures/docs/2012/Forest Facts_1952-2012_English.pdf.

United States Department of Agriculture, United States Forest Service. "Discover the Forest." www.discovertheforest.org.

Watson, Geraldine Ellis. *Reflections on the Neches: A Naturalist's Odyssey Along the Big Thicket's Snow River.* Denton: Big Thicket Association and University of Texas Press, 2003.

Watson, Geraldine Ellis. *Big Thicket Plant Ecology: An Introduction.* 3rd ed. Denton: Big Thicket Association and University of North Texas Press, 2006.

Wessels, Tom. *Reading the Forested Landscape: A Natural History of New England.* Woodstock, VT: The Countryman Press, 1997.

Wessels, Tom. *Forest Forensics: A Field Guide to Reading the Forested Landscape.* New York: The Countryman Press, 2010.

Whitney, Ellie, D. Bruce Means, and Anne Rudloe. *Priceless Florida: Natural Ecosystems and Native Species.* Sarasota, FL: Pineapple Press, 2004.

Wojtech, Michael. *Bark: A Field Guide to Trees of the Northwest.* Hanover and London: University Press of New England, 2011.

INDEX

Index

Pacific silver fir, *228*

Pando (aspen forest in Utah), 17

Paynes Prairie Preserve State Park (Florida), 8

petrichor, 12

photosynthesis, 36, 37–38, 89, 103

pigs, wild, 107, 116–17

pileated woodpeckers, 51, *111*, 111–12, 125

pill bugs, 155

pine, 11, 30. *See also* conifers

pine species: jack, 31; longleaf, 54, 121, 125–26, 163–64; pitch, 34, 37; ponderosa, 164; red, 31; singleleaf pinyon, 31; sugar, 31–32; white, 21–22, 23–24, 31, 39, 192

pinecones (cones), 7, 31–32, 121–22, 160

pine tar, 54

Pioneer Mothers Memorial Forest (Indiana), 193

pitch pine, 34, 37

poison ivies, 13

poison oak, 13

Polaris (Viking longboat), 201

pollen, 11, 98. *See also* reproduction

ponderosa pine, 164

poplar, 17, 33, 74

porcupines, 51, 117, 121, 151–52

possums (opossums), 121, 123, 187

rabies, 123

raccoons, 51, 66, 121, 123, 187

rain, 11, 105–6, 143–44. *See also* water

ramps (wild leeks), 153

rats, 19

red-backed salamanders, 134

red cedar, 31. *See also* cedar

red-cockaded woodpeckers, 125–27

red light, 87–88

red maple, 33

red pine, 31

red spruce, 18

redwood, *x*, 22, 24–25, 28, 141. *See also* giant sequoia

reindeer moss, 44

reproduction: fungi, 59, 106; mosses, 48–49; trees, 11–12, 101

resin, 10, 54, 71–72, 98, 160–61

respiration, 37–38, 88

resurrection fern, 47

rings, tree, 53–54

roots: introduction, 19; animals and, 19; interconnectedness, 17; longevity of, 16–17; purposes of, 14–15, 16; safety around, 14; soil and, 15–16, 17–19; water and, 16, 18

ruffed grouse, 59

salamanders, 56, 132–35

sapsuckers, 40, 124–25

scaly deadwood beetles, 137–38

scars, 38–41

scat, 119

scavenging activity, 82–84

scents, 9–12, 73–74

seasons: introduction, 95; fall, 105–7; spring, 96–102; summer, 103–5; winter, 95–96

shoes and boots, 180–81

sight: night vision, 87–88; sense of, 8–9

silver maple, 33

Pacific silver fir cone, Maple Pass, Washington

ABOUT
THE AUTHORS

PETER WOHLLEBEN studied at the University of Applied Forest Sciences in Rottenburg before working for the Rhineland-Palatinate state forestry commission. After twenty-three years as a government employee, he resigned so he could implement his vision of environmentally responsible forest management through a forest academy he founded in Wershofen, Germany. Peter also travels internationally to support the defenders of old-growth forests. His passion—after the trees themselves—is teaching people about the wonders to be found in forests and about the crucial role trees play in making life possible on this planet. His books are bestsellers in countries around the world.

JANE BILLINGHURST is a nature enthusiast, master gardener, editor, translator, and author of six books. She has translated and edited several books by Peter Wohlleben, including the *New York Times* bestseller *The Hidden Life of Trees*. For this book, she took a four-month trip visiting forests around North America including giant redwoods in California, piney woods in Texas, bottomland forests in southeastern states, deciduous forests reclaiming agricultural land in the northeast, and the boreal forest in Quebec. She lives next to 2,800 acres of community forest lands in Anacortes, Washington, where she regularly walks under Douglas firs, red cedars, and hemlocks.

Jane would like to thank the following people who shared their expertise with her on her journey: David Lee, leaf expert at Florida International University, forest entomologist and Viking boat builder Torolf Torgersen, and forester and fellow master gardener Alison Hitchcock, all of whom provided valuable feedback on the text; Max Harper, Big Thicket National Preserve, Texas; Holly Platz, environmental educator at Guadalupe River State Park, Texas; Susan and Brian Woodworth, volunteer educators at Highlands Hammock State Park, Florida; Elijah W. Kruger, environmental educator, Letchworth State Park, New York; and Sarada Sangameswaran, education director, Pittsburgh Botanic Garden, Pennsylvania.